THE
LAW SCHOOL
RULES

115 SURVIVAL STRATEGIES
TO MAKE THE CHALLENGES OF
LAW SCHOOL SEEM LIKE
"SMALL STUFF"

MARION T.D. LEWIS

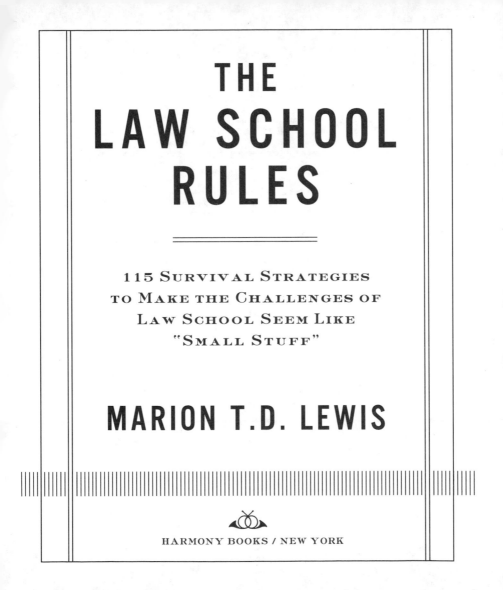

HARMONY BOOKS / NEW YORK

DEDICATED
TO MY MOTHER AND FATHER

Published by Harmony Books, 201 East 50th Street, New York, New York 10022.
Member of the Crown Publishing Group.

Random House, Inc. New York, Toronto, London, Sydney, Auckland
www.randomhouse.com

HARMONY Books is a registered trademark and
Harmony Books colophon is a trademark of
Random House, Inc.

Originally published by The Waterfall Press in 1998.
Copyright © 1998 by T. D. Lewis

Printed in the United States of America

DESIGN BY KAREN MINSTER

Library of Congress Cataloging-in-Publication Data

Lewis, Marion T. D.
The law school rules: 115 survival strategies to make the
challenges of law school seem like small stuff / Marion T.D. Lewis.
—1st ed.
Includes bibliographical references.
(hc)
1. Law—Study and teaching—United States.   2. Law students—United States.   I. Title.
KF283.L49   1999   340'.071'173—dc21   99-30266

ISBN 0-609-60528-3

10 9 8 7 6 5 4 3 2 1

First Harmony Books Edition

CONTENTS

PART THREE: Study Tips for Everybody!

PART FOUR: Professors

PART FIVE: Do's and Don'ts

PART SIX: Health and Coping

PART SEVEN: Money Tips

PART EIGHT: Networking, Suits, and Jobs

PART NINE: Simple Pleasures

ACKNOWLEDGMENTS

First, I thank God for the countless blessings He has bestowed upon me.

Next, eternal gratitude to my family—my mother and father, Vernie and Wycliffe Lewis; my siblings, niece, and nephews: Bridget, Angella, Monica, Johann, Charlene, Jennifer, Shika, Jawaan, Jono, and Stefan; and of course, to my cat, Bachanalia. Without their love and support, I couldn't have done any of this.

Thanks to my dearest friends: Joseph Maniangatt for his love, friendship, and emotional support (which kept me sane throughout my law school years) and for continuing to keep me sane every day; Michael P. Ryan, my long-time friend, and the unwitting instrument through whom I gained the insight for writing this book; and my girlfriends, Monica Mahan, Manisha Patel, and Matilda Roman for their undying enthusiasm for my writing in general, and *The Law School Rules* in particular, and for being my buddies. Thanks, guys!

Samuel Musora, my great friend, introduced me to Saki Mafundikwa at the Crown Publishing Group, and Saki indirectly led me to Ayesha Pande, who led me to PJ Dempsey—the editor to whom I owe the greatest thanks. I thank Samuel for boosting my writing career. He came through for me once again, and I do appreciate it so much. I also appreciate how much he's made me laugh in the last few months.

Speaking of Ayesha Pande . . . Had she not humored me that morning back in September 1998, when I called her cold, asking her to allow me to send her a copy of my self-published book, I would never have met PJ Dempsey. So thanks, Ayesha! And thanks to PJ Dempsey for taking a chance on me, an unknown writer. With her guidance, I was able to polish *The Law School Rules* into a work fit for the national market. I am deeply indebted to her. I also thank all the other players at Crown, such as Elizabeth Bird, thank you from the bottom of my heart for giving *The Law School Rules* a new lease on life.

I'm extremely grateful to the following people who read the original version of the book and gave me feedback on how to improve it: Eric Kochel, Christopher Waldron, Professor Peter Zablotsky of New York Law School, Vernie Lewis, Wycliffe Lewis, and Matilde Roman. I also acknowledge Professor Stephen J. Ellmann for helping me to articulate how to "think like a lawyer"; Professor Elaine Mills, who took the time one day to offer me advice on different steps I might take; Professor Martin Levin, who helped me with certain contractual matters; the Public Relations Department at New York Law School for promoting the book; and Michael Dwyer in the New York Law School Bookstore for his selling and promotional help. I also acknowledge Dorothy Spencer in the New York Law School accounting office, for always greeting me with a smile when I was a student there.

Finally, Emad Owaid, Jennifer Langdon, Ann Cammett, and Giovanni Ramirez were instrumental in helping me with the original version of the book. Had I not had their professional help, I may not have been able to create a product, as I did, that attracted the attention of a major publishing company like the Crown Publishing Group. Thus, I thank them all.

INTRODUCTION

If you are like me, you were probably an above-average student in college, and you think you can handle law school just as easily. What you will quickly learn is that while law school is, simply, a step up from college in most cases, it has a climate all of its own that requires proper acclimation if you are to succeed as a law student.

The Law School Rules, which I wrote for you (so that you don't make the same mistakes I did), came about as a result of important lessons I learned after a particularly horrendous 1L (first year of law school) experience. One crucial lesson was that while many things that contributed to my unpleasant beginning in law school were outside my "locus of control," a large part of my problem was self-sabotage—and this was very much within my "locus of control."

Self-sabotage occurs when you fail to follow certain fundamental rules. But you will not make the same mistakes, or break as many rules, as I and some of your predecessors did—because you will know *The Law School Rules*. This book is my gift to you. It is light, informative, and geared specifically at arming you with tools for handling the "small stuff" of law school—which, if left unattended, can quickly mushroom into "big stuff," and potentially affect your ability to concentrate, study, and maximize your grades. But the emphasis here isn't on grades. While grades *are* important in law school (almost as important, for instance, as the contacts one has), the over-emphasis on grades in many of the other books on the subject of law school, and the lack of emphasis on the other intangibles and minutiae that can affect a student's life—and thus their performance in law school—fails, in my opinion, to effectively equip law students such as yourself with workable tips on how to deal.

It's never the "big stuff" in law school that will throw your life out of balance and cause you to feel unhappy or unproductive (which, in turn, can cause a slump in your grades). It's the "small stuff" that will get to you every time and eat away at your confidence like worms. That's why I've set out to be a part of the solution to what I view as a dearth of information for law students who don't want to be plum loco three years down the road, but who want to do well and still maintain inner harmony. Yes, there is a link between inner harmony and success in law school. If you are to be a successful law student, you must strive to be a happy, balanced, and productive person. This, in turn, will naturally lead to a maximization of your academic performance. It's that simple.

The Rules is for you if you're thinking about entering, are just starting, or are already in law school and want some pointers on making yours a better law school experience. Though there's a full section of study hints, these are only a fraction of the ideas covered. *The Rules* touches on every aspect of your law school experience from eating well, to investing in a computer, to budgeting and sticking to a financial plan, to forming study groups, to using commercial outlines, to using aromatherapy as a memory enhancer, to knowing how to handle sexual harassment, and much, much more.

The operative word in this book is "balance." The operative phrase is "do what's best for you." As long as you remember these tenets, you will do just fine.

Remember, always, that I wrote this book when I was where you are now—in 1L (the first year of law school). As a result, the pain, the humiliation, the fear—all of the experiences—were still raw and fresh in my mind. I know what you're feeling. I can relate to your insecurities—much better than a professor who has been out of law school for twenty years.

This is what you should do: Read this book in its entirety. Follow the rules! Refer back to them throughout 1L when you need a picker-upper or a reminder. The information is practical, simple, and realistic. Following the rules will make your transition from sane human being to law student less daunting. And this in turn will lead to your ultimate success. I promise.

1

IT ALL BEGINS IN YOUR MIND

DARE TO BE GREAT

> It is far better to dare mighty things,
> to win glorious triumphs, even though
> checkered by failure, than take rank
> with those poor spirits who neither
> enjoy much nor suffer much, because
> they live in the gray twilight that
> knows not victory nor defeat . . .
>
> —Theodore Roosevelt

Some people might say that getting through law school is like getting to the top of Mount Kilimanjaro. Most days it'll be tough—an uphill climb with you puffing, sweating, and choking all the way. Others might say that law school is like running an obstacle course and barely getting over all the hurdles. Still others might say that law school is a jungle where only the fittest survive.

In spite of it all, it's a fact that most people who attempt law school survive it. Thus, the odds of you surviving are overwhelmingly in your favor. You'll succeed if you have gumption, guts, ambition, self-confidence, and daring. And it won't hurt if you're a little bit crazy, too. And, remember that anything worth having is worth working hard for.

In the beginning, there will be days when you'll feel like you're in the "gray twilight." You may even think defeat is inevitable when you find yourself responding to a professor's questions with the proverbial "er, um, huh?" before drawing a complete blank, while the chump next to you is rattling off the facts of the case as if this individual authored the Opinion.

This is normal. It's at this crucial beginning stage that the seeds of self-doubt will begin to plant their ugly roots in your mind, play havoc with your psyche, and upset your ever-so-fragile equilibrium. Whatever you do, don't allow these seeds to germinate. Do not! You're no "poor spirit." You will not "take rank" with anybody but those who move on to 2L, to 3L, and then to graduation. Still, if you're like most law students, your journey may be "checkered by (tiny) failures" like a not-so-good grade in a class for which you studied your heart out. Don't worry. There will be many triumphs worth celebrating—like a good grade, mastering the art of doing an IRAC analysis (see Rule 44), or giving such a great answer in class that not only do you astound the professor and your fellow classmates, but you also shock the pants (literally!) off yourself as well.

Remember: Every triumph counts. Pat yourself on the back

for each job well done—even if nobody else does. And in spite of the tiny failures, never give up striving to be the best law school student you can be.

As Theodore Roosevelt correctly pointed out, "it's far better to dare mighty things" than not to. And make no mistake about it: Getting through law school is a mighty deed to dare and a mighty deed to do. But it's entirely do-able. And it's a lot more do-able if you immerse yourself in it. Go on! The idea isn't to lose yourself completely. Just don't fight every step of the way.

Think of it this way: You're Jonah. Law school is the whale. One way or another, you're going down into the whale's belly (whether you like it or not). Now, you can go down "whole" and get spit out "whole" three years down the road; or, you can fight the whale, get chewed into pieces, and get spit out in bits three years down the road. What's it going to be?

BELIEVE IN YOURSELF

Don't ever allow anything or anyone to stop you from believing in yourself. And this goes for everybody—including peers and professors, but especially the latter. Professors can be tough on a law student's ego. But try to remember that one professor's opinion of you or your work does not your legal career make. If you're good, you're good. And with time, you'll be even better. Nothing and nobody can change that. Especially not a professor who probably isn't being objective.

Here's a story you might find encouraging. It's the story of a law student who got a D in Torts during his first year of law school. Of course he was crushed and felt like a failure. Years later, by an ironic twist of fate, that student became an obscenely successful personal injury attorney. With some of the money he acquired throughout his celebrated career, the student bought, among other things, a townhouse in an exclusive part of town. One day, this student decided to throw a bash. He invited "everybody who was anybody," and was sure to invite the professor who gave him a D in Torts . . . How delicious is this so far?

Anyhow, sometime during the course of the evening the student finally managed to have a few words with the professor. Looking around to survey all the material wealth he had acquired as a personal injury attorney, the student turned to the professor and whispered: "This is what a D in Torts will get you!"

Revenge is sweet, isn't it? The moral of the story is, never stop believing in yourself no matter what anybody tells you. Everybody's playing a mind game in law school. They're all trying to psych you out. Especially your professors. Don't let them play with your head. The minute you start to doubt yourself you're in trouble. Big trouble. So, if no one else believes you can get to the top of Kilimanjaro (see Rule 1), you must never stop believing in yourself. Stay focused on why you're in law school in the first place. Everyone has their reasons. Don't lose sight of yours.

And always keep in mind that you've done the legwork. You've graduated from college with a four-year degree. You've prepared for and taken the LSAT. You've applied to and been accepted to law school. You're not an idiot. You're the same intelligent human being you were before you met these people (peers and professors) who are trying their darndest to convince you that you're not as smart, and never will be as smart, as they are. You've earned your spot in law school, my friend. You can do it! Besides, it's not about what any of these people think. *What do you think?* That's the real question.

THINK THE THOUGHT

Successfully completing law school is very much a case of mind over matter. It's all about believing in yourself, right? Well, yes, but you'll have to do a little bit more. Not only do you have to believe in yourself, you'll have to "think the thought" as well.

What does that mean? "Thinking the thought" means that you've got to see the futility of worrying and obsessing about things you have no control over. Simply think and believe the process will work for you in the end, that whatever makes the forces of the universe "tick" will take care of you and that everything will work out exactly the way it should. Once you start thinking this way, you'll automatically begin to take care of whatever is within your "locus of control." Then everything will fall nicely into place.

WALK THE WALK

After you've "thunk the thought," it's time to physically take care of everything within your locus of control. In other words, it's time to "walk the walk" to a successful completion of your goal—graduating from law school. Graduating is not a fairy tale. You must take action. The forces of the universe will help you only if you help yourself!

So get off your buns and get to work. Keep your eyes (for that matter your entire being) on the path to the prize of successfully moving on to the second year, then the third year, and then on to the grand prix—graduation!

Perseverance is key. This implies a host of things. For example, you'll have to attend classes regularly and pay keen attention; you'll have to keep up with your reading; and continue to brief your cases throughout the semester. If possible, you may want to tape your classes and have regular meetings with your study group (if you choose to join one) to brainstorm and compare notes.

Walking the walk also means having a sense of humor, a sense of balance, a sense of objectivity, and good friends. It means maintaining good physical and mental health by exercising, eating right, saying no to drugs and alcohol, and engaging regularly in activities that reduce stress and strengthen your body and mind. It also means understanding the importance of taking "time out" from time to time, maybe engaging in a hobby, getting yourself a pet, throwing a get-together, making whoopie with that special someone, or in some way indulging in the simpler pleasures of life.

You may also find that developing good communication skills—with family members, a significant other, roommates, or anyone who could affect your ability to concentrate and study—is well worth your time. It will make your life (and your law school experience) so much easier.

Get over the
Law School Mystique

The law school mystique—that is, thinking of law school as phenomenally difficult, utterly mind-boggling, and wholly mysterious—can be crippling. Get over it. It's just law school! Think of law school as being a mere step up from college. Nothing more. Don't get wrapped up in your own fallacious ideas of what law school should be. When you're all wrapped up in knots like that, it's counterproductive. Deal with what law school is, instead. Again, it's just a step up from college—the boot camp of the legal profession. Say that to yourself over and over. Convince yourself it's true.

If you can convince yourself of this you're well on your way to becoming a good lawyer. Lawyers by necessity not only have to convince themselves of "stuff," they often have to convince others as well. This ability literally pays the rent. So practice on yourself. Start now. Convince yourself that law school is no big deal. Get over that silly law school mystique!

RULE 6

Do Away with Your Common Sense and "Think Like a Lawyer"

Check your common-sense reactions to the law and law school at the door. This will lower your levels of frustration. Law school is sometimes counterintuitive. In other words, there often seems to be no logic to it all. The Rule? Don't expect everything to make sense. Sometimes nothing will. Let go of your "logical way of thinking." Stop thinking like a layperson. You are no longer a layperson. You're a lawyer-to-be. Think like a lawyer.

What does it mean to "think like a lawyer"? Excellent question. There have been books written on the subject. Yet an explanation remains elusive. Some people (even nonlawyers) are said to just have the knack for this way of thinking. For others, thinking like a lawyer is counterintuitive. For how do lawyers think? Does it mean giving up one's own values? How does one even explain how to think like a lawyer? It isn't easy, but here goes: Lawyers think subtly, deeply, and precisely. They're full of contradictions: for example, they're at once sensitive, brutish, quick-thinking, nit-picking human beings. Like detectives, they often have to out-think criminals. And golly, can they ever connive! They have the ability to tie you up in mental knots, and when they're through with you, all that's left of you is the orange juice you had for *yesterday's* breakfast. Lawyers are cunning. They understand that everything is open to interpretation and are able to read between lines, to see things that are not perfectly clear to the "ordinary person."

Lawyers understand and cultivate the art of listening and spinning facts in such a way that the impossible becomes the truth—and they get others to believe them. They have the ability to get any word (preposition, conjunction, gerund, you name it!) or fact to work for them. They have an incredible gift of gab. They are able to hallucinate rationally, make the illogical sensical, see mirages—yet they are able to convince you that what they're seeing is real. Lawyers are sanely delusional. They are analytical, intuitive, and mad . . . And you, my friend, have to become just like them. Because the quicker you can start "thinking like a lawyer," the less hellish your law school experience will be.

KEEP YOUR CHIN UP

For every situation there's a worse situation. It could be a lot worse than having to spend three years of your life in a legal institution trying to figure out how to think like a lawyer. No, really! You could be in a mental institution eating biscuits with a guy named Pearl. You could be a high-school drop-out. You could be homeless. You could be doing hard labor in Siberia. Or worse.

So whenever you feel like hanging your head in despair, remember that somewhere out there at least one person would trade places with you in a heartbeat. After all, you got accepted to law school. Many apply but few are chosen. You are one of the chosen ones, my friend! You're special. So count yourself lucky and keep your chin up!

SWIM WITH THE TIDE, NOT AGAINST IT

Prepare to feel like you're back in grade school. The autonomy you had in college is a thing of the past in law school. You give up a lot of control in law school, especially in 1L (the first year). In fact, an argument can be made that you give up *all* control in the first year of law school. You don't get to choose the classes that you'll take or your professors. Nor will you be able to prepare your own class schedule. Often, you don't even get to choose where you sit in the classroom. Is it any wonder there's so much regressive behavior among first-year law students? First-years are treated like children! What with professors ranting and raving the way your parents did when you failed to clean up your room! Oh, how 1Ls fear law professors.

What to do? Don't fight. Swim with the tide, not against it. 1L is just another rite of passage. It, too, will pass. Soon you'll be a 2L. And by 3L, all you'll want is your J.D. So don't think of your right to be treated as an adult. Instead, think of survival every step of the way.

Filter Out the Garbage

Filter out all the law school crap that everyone—mostly your fellow (terrified!) classmates—will try to fill your head with. Yes, you've probably read Scott Turow's *One L* and you've seen the movie *The Paper Chase*. But no professor is going to "give you a quarter to call your mother" (it's not Hollywood, it's just law school). And if he does, politely tell him you have your own cell phone and/or phone card.

Also, if certain individuals make you feel particularly nervous and negative, avoid them. You can't afford the luxury of hanging around nervous wrecks or negative classmates. Before you know it you could become just like them. Remember the old adage, "you're known by the company you keep"? Take that a step further to "you become the company you keep."

Find a Sense of Balance

You'll need to learn to balance LIVING with being a law student, unless you want law school to be anything but pure hell. This is the ultimate Rule. Learn to balance studying with things unrelated to case books—fun things for your own relaxation—like playing a half hour of frisbee with your dog, painting, having a conversation with your significant other, having a nice meal, working out, or whatever it is that turns you on.

This is your life. Who knows where you'll be and what you'll be doing three years down the road. Live in the moment—and this is a rule for life in general, not just life in law school. But given the stresses you'll experience in law school, living in the moment takes on an even greater sense of urgency; so don't put off all your pleasure till you graduate! Besides, taking breaks from your books and balancing study time with leisure time actually serves a greater purpose. You'll feel replenished once you've taken time out, so that when you go back to your books, you'll be able to accomplish a lot more.

Dare to Relax

While you're busy daring to be great (see Rule 1), you must also learn to relax. Stop. RELAX. Smell the roses. Get a soothing massage. In fact, *dare to relax* should be your mantra. Take lots of deep breaths. Everything will be just fine. BREATHE. Don't let anybody psych you out. There will always be people who will try to intimidate you intellectually, as well as in other ways. They'll give you the impression that they know a lot more than you, or that they're more entitled to be in law school than you, all because their daddy is a big shot, and your daddy, well, he shines the big shot's shoes (as if that has anything to do with it!). It's a mind game, my friend. Don't let them play with your head. Relax. Relax. Relax.

VISUALIZE WHAT YOU WANT

Psych yourself up. How, you wonder, can you do this when all you see is academic catastrophe looming hideously ahead? Use visualization techniques.

You'll be better able to maximize the benefits of visualization when you're relaxed and unhurried. So select about ten minutes each day. A good time is right before going to bed. (Also see Rule 13.) Imagine that whatever it is you *want* you already *have*. No, it's not crazy! Eventually, you'll start living the thought. Experts claim that when you picture what you want in your mind, you're more likely to get it. So do it. Picture yourself with your degree in hand. Savor the taste of this accomplishment. Let it moisten your hungry palate.

Picture yourself working in a law firm. Or "kicking butt" in front of a jury. Now, picture yourself in the moment. You're in law school, relaxed, and enjoying the experience. Keep telling yourself: "Moment by moment, I will get where I want to go." Before you know it, you'll be smiling a lot more, but also looking forward to getting to class, maybe participating in class discussions and getting a better understanding of the law and the way it works. You might even be on your way to better grades than you expected. You never know.

TRY THIS VISUALIZATION EXERCISE

If you're finding it hard to let up a bit, do this: Imagine you have an egg in your hands. A delicate bird's egg. It has much potential. You don't want to break this egg. You want to protect it, so that it can realize its potential.

Your first instinct might be to hold the egg really tight. Right? That's what we all do when we want to protect something. And the more scared of dropping it you become, the tighter you hold it. What do you think will happen? Bingo! You see, holding on really tight, or trying really, really hard (example, studying so hard and long your face hurts) isn't always the best way. Sometimes a looser, lighter grasp is better. Sometimes putting the egg (or book) down for a rest is best. Otherwise all you might end up with is a crushed mess.

Remember: Making the transition to law school isn't easy. But when the going gets tough—as it will—know that hundreds of thousands before you got through it and so will you. You'll live! A little bit of moxie, a light grasp, and a visual image of what you want and where you want to go will take you a long way. Keep visualizing what you want. If you can picture it, you can make it come true. (Now re-read Rule 12.)

SAVOR THE LUXURY OF
BEING A STUDENT

Law students who don't take time off between college and law school tend to want to rush through law school so they can get out in the real world and start making money. What a shame! Don't you realize that three extra years out of the real world is a luxury?! Enjoy the luxury of being a student! Quell the urge to rush through law school. It will go by quickly enough.

If you're busy trying to rush through it, it will feel a lot longer than it really is, and your frustration levels will mount. Then what would be the point? Think about it: You'll have over forty years of your life left to work and do other things. God only knows those years will probably crawl, or be filled with taking care of family, career, and all the rest of it. So enjoy your freedom. Luxuriate in it. Savor it. Relish it. Believe it or not, these *are* the good old days.

Do What's Best for You

You are a unique human being in every way—including the way you react to and handle the challenges of law school. Thus, you must figure out what's best for you—you'll learn through trial and error—and do just that.

For example, law students, by necessity, have to carry heavy casebooks all the time. But just because most students carry knapsacks doesn't mean that a knapsack is best for YOU—especially if you've always had a bad back. While you can't use a shopping cart (and there will be days you wish you could!), a shoulder bag or a briefcase-on-wheels could be the next best thing. Or maybe you need to distribute the weight by using two bags—one for your shoulder, the other for your opposite hand . . . You may think this is a trivial point, but it's not. A sore back can cause missed days of school; it could be so distracting that even if you're physically in class the only thing you'll be able to think about is your pain.

There are myriad ways in which you could differ from your classmates. Like whether or not a study group will work for you; like whether you should tape-record your classes, and so on. You don't necessarily have to follow the masses. You know yourself best. DO WHAT'S BEST FOR YOU.

2

FIRST-YEAR
BASICS

Wear What Is Comfortable for You

As far as dressing for law school, wear what is comfortable for you. (Again you should do what's best for you. See Rule 15.) But don't feel that because you're in law school you should look "serious" or worse, unkempt, all the time. Save dingy sweats for weekends and suits for special occasions—such as interviews, networking events, or jobs.

A nice, clean pair of jeans, no matter what your size, is a must. You can also wear slacks, shorts, khakis, skirts, whatever. Be chic. Be young. Play up your assets. You'll feel better about yourself and you won't resent others who you might think look breezier, perkier, younger, or (gasp!) happier and bubblier. Don't resent 'em! Join 'em! Chances are they're just doing the best they can with what they've got and so should you. When you look your best you're more likely to feel your best, and when you feel your best, law school will feel a lot less hellish.

Take Care of Paperwork

Make sure all your paperwork for the registrar, admissions, financial aid, and whatever other offices need "paper" (everybody is paper-crazy in law school) is in order by the first day of class. It'll make law school easier.

For example, did you fill out all the forms in your financial-aid packet, complete with copies of yours and your parents' tax forms? More specifically, is your grant-in-aid information, scholarship applications, Tuition Assistance Application, and all other financial-aid paperwork taken care of? Are they complete? That is, did you get all the needed signatures—namely yours, your spouse's (if married), and your parents'? Did you send for all post–high school transcripts from schools you've attended? (For some reason the registrar always seems to need extra copies of transcripts.) Make sure you've answered all these questions and any others resoundingly in the affirmative. Be a pest if you must. Call the registrar's, admissions and financial-aid offices to double, triple, and quadruple check that all your paperwork is in order. You'll be glad you did.

SHAKE THE JITTERS

To tremble or not to tremble? That's the question on the lips of many first-year law students. Your first day of law school will probably be an orientation of some kind. (You'll never feel as nervous as this again, thank God!) The rule is, go ahead and tremble. Shake those jitters. Get them out of your system once and for all.

During orientation, try to observe one other student. Why? Just note your perceptions of that person based solely on their appearance. To the extent you can, keep track of this person over time. It doesn't have to be someone of the opposite sex, although that might be fun. It could be someone of another racial group, or someone older, or someone who looks like a snob, or anybody.

As the semester progresses, see whether your visual impressions were right. As a matter of fact, why not observe them for the three years of law school? How did this person impact your experience? Does this person make really "stupid" comments in class when they had looked smart to you? Or do they make "brilliant" comments when they had looked dumb to you? Or perhaps they didn't impact you at all?

What's the point? Well, all of us have, at one time or another, prejudged someone based solely on that person's outward appearance. (Unfortunately, some things don't change in law school.) But the old adage "never judge a book by its cover" is worth keeping in mind. Perception really isn't everything. So give people a chance.

Listen Keenly to What Is Said at Orientation

During orientation the Dean, a few professors, and upperclass students will tell you about the school and the legal profession in general. They will inform you that if you want to get filthy rich, law school probably isn't the place. Especially given the fact that, going into the new millennium, the number of law graduates in the United States alone is expected to skyrocket well into the millions!

The speakers will tell you things like the legal profession is "self-policing" ("huh?" you say) and mention something about how technology is changing the role of lawyers in society. ("Oh God, will I find a job?!" you say.) The speakers will extol the ethical responsibility of being a good, honest lawyer. ("Oxymoron!" shout the lay people).

The speakers will probably mention the importance of study groups and not falling behind in your reading, among other things. They're also likely to emphasize the importance of respecting the points of view of your fellow classmates even though you might disagree.

One of the speakers will probably also talk about the glass-ceiling phenomenon, racism, sexual harassment, and other issues that usually affect women and members of minority groups but can affect others as well. Listen to everything that is said, even if you happen to be male and/or majority, or even if you're fully convinced that these problems are just figments of other people's imaginations. Maybe by being open you'll see or hear something you weren't aware of before, something that could have a huge impact on the kind of lawyer you'll end up being.

Don't Judge Your Classmates

The ability to analyze and make determinations based on evidence versus making assumptions based on the way something or someone looks is important in law school, as well as in life. Don't judge. The very person you snubbed because they looked brain-dead might be able to help you one day when you're standing clueless in the library trying to get started on your legal-research project.

If you must judge another, then judge them on the basis of their character. For, if you don't want people to make terrible assumptions about you, you shouldn't be making terrible assumptions about them. Every white person is not a racist. Some are wonderful human beings and this irrational way of thinking could cause you to miss out on some really good friends. Every black person does not need quotas and "affirmative action" to get into law school. Some are brilliant, accomplished, well-schooled individuals who might even have higher GPA's and LSAT scores than you do. Some women have naturally large breasts and (not that it's any of your business even if these glands *were* fake). So don't make a fool of everybody concerned by thinking that a woman's body parts define her intelligence, because she may be *way* smarter than you. And, finally, all men are not pigs.

Isn't it time, anyway, that our social discourse—both inside and outside the classroom—is elevated to a higher level than the same tired, old, conversations, stereotypes, and cliches? Stereotypes and cliches not only stifle, poison, and bog down those around you, they affect your individual life and/or your law school experience as well. You see, the universe is a circle. And what goes around comes around. So if you're stifling, poisoning, and bogging down others, eventually it comes back to you. And if you're judging others, then judgment will eventually fall back on you.

BE NICE, BE HAPPY

When the average person thinks of lawyers, words like aggressive, mean, stressed, fighting, and strong probably come to mind a lot quicker than nice or happy. Because you're being groomed to be a lawyer, these same people (or even you) may think you have to take on these qualities in order to gain respect. That's why if you ask the average layperson, they'll probably say that a nice or happy lawyer is an oxymoron.

Still others believe that law students should be serious all the time. And it seems as if some law students think that being serious means not being nice. For them, niceness equals weakness, and being weak means being a loser. In other words, you can't be "too nice" in law school if you want to be taken "seriously." And law students who fit that "nice" mold can quickly get the reputation of being bimbos or push-overs, they'll be disliked or ridiculed, or they'll get completely taken for granted because, as the saying goes, "nice guys finish last." Well, somebody's got to stop this madness!

Law school is hard enough without having to worry that you seem too happy, too nice, or not serious enough to your peers. That doesn't mean you should be a fake or be a doormat to those who try to take advantage of you (as will often happen). But what's the point of living if you think that life is not only short, it's miserable, serious, stressful, and unhappy, and all you see on the horizon are casebooks and professors who think your IQ is lower than his two-year-old?

If you can maintain a nice, happy disposition in a law school environment you'll be the fittest of the law school survivors. For it takes tremendous fitness to maintain such a disposition when all around you is gloom, doom, seriousness, and people who want to tear you apart simply because you're "too happy, perky, or bubbly." How easy it is to get caught up in all that! But don't. It's not worth it. Dare to be happy, darn it! There's no rule that says law students can't laugh at the top of their lungs. Hey, laughter is sexy! So laugh. Laugh plenty. Have a personality. Be a good human being.

Remember, too, that nice and happy human beings live longer. They get fewer heart attacks and they're more attractive because they don't get angry lines and wrinkles in their faces from grimacing all the time. And, when you feel happy inside, it shows on the outside. And hey, nice, happy (a.k.a. attractive), law students become nice, happy (a.k.a. attractive) lawyers. So there!

Do Your Assignments and Protect Your Confidence

You can't cut corners with assignments in 1L. It will come back to haunt you. Doing your assignments *every time* makes law school easier, and protects your confidence from being shattered by a professor who catches you unprepared!

You should have gotten a schedule of classes in the mail at least a couple of weeks before the first day of class. Find out what books have been assigned by each professor. Buy your books right away. Start reading.

In fact, this is what you should do: A week or two before your first day of class, go to your school to check the bulletin board for your class assignments. Assignments are usually listed by professor. These days, many schools have computerized bulletin boards, so you don't even have to stand in line. You can stay across the room and read a jumbo screen suspended above even the tallest person's head. Or you can call an automated phone line and punch in a code and get your assignments while sitting on your bed. However, if your school is still in the technological Dark Ages, it behooves you to go to your school, stand in line if you have to, and find out what your assignments are.

The point is, you have to stay on top of what is assigned even before the first day of class. Remember, law school is a bit different from college in this respect: Professors expect you to check the bulletin board for your assignment *before* classes begin. On the first day of class, a professor could call on you and expect you to be prepared to tell them the facts of what's bound to be a complicated case. (Yes, I agree. It's completely insane!) The other students will be only too glad they weren't the ones called on. They'll be content to sit and listen to you mumble incomprehensibly about nothing. They might even secretly gloat if you make a fool of yourself, especially if you haven't bothered to do your assignment.

Were you to get caught unprepared this early in the game, it could be detrimental to your law school career because you could lose your confidence (over something that is totally avoidable!). Then you'll find yourself in the unenviable position of spending the rest of your time trying to prove you're not a slacker or moron. But the damage would have already been done because your confidence would have been shattered, and confidence is *everything* in law school. It truly is the secret of success. So always do your assignments, if only to safeguard your confidence.

FOLLOW THE SYLLABUS

After the first day of class, the professor will usually give out a syllabus. Follow this syllabus carefully. Prepare for class every single day. Don't leave anything out. If possible, skim the footnotes. Chances are, if the professor took the time to put something on the syllabus, he plans on going over it. (Law professors tend to be sticklers for details.)

Oh, by the way, the method the professor uses to conduct the lecture is called the Socratic Method. The Socratic Method apparently helps to make you "literate as a lawyer." It teaches you to "think and talk like a lawyer." Remember: The quicker you learn to "think and talk like a lawyer" (see Rule 6), the less hellish your experience will be.

Be Warned about the "Socratic Method"

If you're in 1L, you're probably asking yourself exactly what is the Socratic Method? It's simply a euphemism for a torturous interrogation. Meaning: The professor who uses this method will stand in front of the class like an over-read, unforgiving drill sergeant and call on some unlucky, terrified sod to give the facts of a case. Then he or she will proceed to grill the poor sod till the poor sod begs for mercy. And that unlucky sod is who? You, of course! You'll be expected to think and speak in a clear, logical way and articulate in lucid detail the convoluted set of facts of the case at bar. More than likely what you'll be doing is a whole host of unprintable things, none of which have anything to do with your thinking and speaking processes. But let's not think about that.

If you did the reading, there are worse fates in law school (like not doing the reading and the professor calling on you) than having to endure a torturous interrogation from a "drill sergeant." The rule: Accept the Socratic Method as a necessary evil. It's another rite of passage you'll have to endure. Yes, it's a tedious, gut-wrenching way of learning the law. Yes, you'll hate it. But, at least, forewarned is forearmed.

Don't Try to Wing It in Your First Year

Law professors are like vampires who take themselves very seriously, and they thrive on the blood of unprepared law students (especially 1Ls) who are naive enough to think they can "wing it." Don't let your professor feast on you. Apply the Boy Scouts' rule: Be prepared! Never go into class unprepared, thinking you can wing it. You can't. Not even if you say ten Hail Marys or your favorite Buddhist chant right before your professor calls on you. You can't wing it! And once your professor smells blood, you're chopped liver.

TALK OR LISTEN?

Let's hear it for the talkers! If they don't participate in class discussions, who will? If you're so inclined, speaking up in class is a nice way to get your grade raised. If you have an opinion and you want it heard, the only way to accomplish it is to open your mouth and say what you have to say. So don't be shy. Speak up!

But you may be not be so inclined. You hate to speak in class and prefer to wait till the professor calls on you—which, to your horror, will happen sooner or later. Or, you're from the school of students who feels that the less they talk, the more they learn. In short, you prefer to listen than to talk. That's fine. There's nothing wrong with being a listener instead of a talker. Silence is golden, right? In fact, there's a certain wisdom to keeping your mouth shut if you so choose. While being a nontalker won't get your grade raised for participation, it has other advantages. You'll probably learn a lot more when you're sitting, watching, and listening than when you're doing all the talking. So if you choose, you can be like the wise owl— narrow-eyed, open-eared, close-mouthed.

Scope Out the Smarty-Pants

There are going to be a few people who seem to know everything from the first day of class. Listening to them, you'll be convinced that if you don't get into a study group with them, you'll flunk out of law school after the first day of 1L. Wrong! The simple fact is that if your classmates were that much smarter than you they wouldn't be in the same law school as you, no matter how smart they sound when they speak. Think about it. If they were *so* much brighter than you, wouldn't they be in Harvard, Yale, or some other Ivy League school? And if they are in an Ivy League school, and you're their classmate, what do they have on you? Nothing. So relax.

Another thing to remember is that these "smarty-pants" are probably just more exposed (for example, their granddaddy, daddy, and mommy are lawyers), are well-read, and/or are using a lot of commercial outlines and hornbooks to master the legalese/lingo they're using to dazzle and baffle you. Read as many of these books as you can. Educate yourself. You, too, can whip yourself into a smarty-pants!

Furthermore, the people who do most of the talking in class (and don't misunderstand, dialogue is good—it's the best-known way to find "truth" in the good old "marketplace") are not necessarily the ones who will end up with top grades. In fact, the top graders and law reviewers, or members of the other journals, are often those you least expect. No, they aren't necessarily the ones who come in every day dressed in Armani or Donna Karen suits. No, they aren't necessarily from the richest, most influential families. Rather, they're probably wearing ratty jeans, or they're sitting quietly in the back looking clueless and bored, and/or they giggle a lot.

But, just because someone is on Law Review or Journal still doesn't necessarily mean they're smarter than you. It's not inconceivable that some of the people on Law Review or Journal will have a lower GPA than you! How is that possible? Did you know that in many law schools, one could "write" one's way to a smarty-pants reputation? By participating in what is called a "write-on" competition, one can catapult one's way to smarty-pants glory. Of course, one's peers will never know the difference if one doesn't tell. They'll assume one graded onto these journals, when, in fact, had it not been for one's superior writing abilities (or well-positioned friends), one might have wound up on academic probation! And who knows how far one can go? If one is liked by one's peers, one could even find oneself elected to a top-notch position—such as editor-in-chief of the *Journal for International and Comparative Law*, or something equally impressive. That would obviously fuel one's confidence. Then one can work really hard on one's grades for the next two years so that one graduates with honors! That way, one's peers will never know that one was never really a "smarty-pants" at all. And, the deception is *fait accompli!* Isn't this brilliant? The lesson here is: Don't worry about flunking out of law school, or not being as smart as everyone else. If you got into law school, chances are, like your so-called "smarty pants" peers, you will succeed in law school.

Always Be Prepared

No matter how diligent a student you are, at one time or another you'll probably be unprepared. There's good news. Some professors don't use the Socratic Method (see Rule 24). To be sure, this group accounts for the minority of American law school professors, because most seem to get a real kick out of torturously interrogating poor, unlucky sods. But there are a few sympathetic professors who find the Socratic Method just as tedious as the sods it's meant to torture. These types take volunteers. So if you must go to class unprepared, take a chance with one of these professors. Otherwise, go to the professor before class starts. Fess up. Hope for good things.

If you don't want to fess up, then it might be better to miss class for that day, go to the library, and catch up on your reading. But this one is totally your call! You may prefer to chance it. Do what you think is best. But don't just sit there and think for one minute that the Dalai Lama can save you from being called on when you know you're unprepared. Unprepared students are magnets for professors. So gambling that your professor won't call on you when you haven't read is a huge gamble. Ever heard of Murphy's Law?

WHEN YOU JUST DON'T KNOW THE ANSWER—ADMIT IT

You've read till way past midnight. You're "prepared." You got enough sleep and arrive at school fresh and ready. Wham! Your professor calls on you, first thing. Ouch. Well, you know the answer to the first question. You feel great. But the drill sergeant starts to grill you. Alas, you haven't the foggiest idea what the answer might be. Is she talking about the same case you've read, you wonder? You break out in a cold sweat.

What to do? Admit you don't know. (What can your professor do at this point, kill you?) But make it clear that you've read the case. Say something like, "Well, what I got from this case was such and such; however, as far as your specific question goes, I'm not altogether sure I interpreted the facts that way . . ." Who is to say your point of view isn't correct?

Of course, the professor might try to embarrass you in spite of your best efforts. Try not to take it to heart. Your professor might have suffered a similar fate in law school and it's her turn. Keep your cool. Speak in a steady, calm voice. Don't you dare feel like a failure for saying: "I'm not sure." After all, who among you (professor included) knows everything?

DON'T GET FRUSTRATED
BY LEGAL WRITING

Legal Writing could be a tough class for you, even if you've always been a "good" writer. But along with legal research, it's probably the most practical skill you'll learn in a law school setting. It's also one of the classes that a lot of law students slack off in. Big mistake. You've got to take this class seriously. It will be very important if you plan on practicing law once you get out in the real world.

Incidentally, don't be disheartened if it take you more than an entire semester to understand what's entailed in legal writing. Like wine, your writing and analytical skills will get better over time. As you write more and more, you'll see an improvement. You may never be Cardozo, but you'll get better with time.

It is true that if someone is a good legal writer, they may score better on exams than you do, even if you "know more law" than they do. But you should still try not to compare yourself to them. The fact is that many law students have spent years working as paralegals before they started law school (lucky them!), and they would obviously have a head start on you as far as understanding what's entailed with legal writing. Don't worry. Eventually, the playing field will level out. Definitely by your second year, you'll know the deal a bit better; and by the third year it'll almost be a cakewalk.

If you're having problems with legal writing, seek help. Check to see whether your school has a writing specialist, or some professional on staff who can help you. These specialists are paid to assist you with your legal writing and you should not be ashamed to seek them out.

LEARN THE SECRET TO
MOOT COURT

The moot-court exercise is usually given in the second semester of your first year of law school. What is "moot court"? It is a court for arguing undecided or hypothetical cases. Basically, it's a drill that enables you to practice your oral advocacy skills: a courtroom drama where you get to persuade a panel of judges (sometimes real judges), through your appellate brief and oral advocacy, that a case should be decided your way. It's pretty safe to assume that all first-year law students will have a moot-court exercise, no matter where you go to law school. And it's understandable that you'll be nervous.

Here's the trick: Know the weakest link in your argument. That's your Achilles' heel. That's what the judges will look for. So figure out beforehand what's weakest about your argument. Have a ready answer or explanation. Like a dog with a bone, hang on to this answer.

Also, know the contents of your brief and your opponent's brief inside out. Have a strong command of the issues, facts, and law that pertain to your particular argument. And be organized. Don't go into your argument with an ocean of papers so deep that you can't find anything. The panel will be throwing questions at you left and right, and you want to be able to quickly find the answers and support your answers with relevant case law. As a matter of fact, it might be better to use index cards instead of pages upon pages of notes. They make a lot less noise and appear to be more organized. (Just don't drop the whole pile of cards the middle of making an important point!)

3

STUDY TIPS FOR EVERYBODY!

FIND AN IDEAL
STUDY ENVIRONMENT

You need a place to study where you are comfortable and able to concentrate.

Where are you going to find this ideal environment? A corner of the library, a reading room, an empty classroom, or your own apartment—which doubles as Shangri-la! (see Rule 107)—or anywhere, except in your bed. Beds are good for many things, but they are the very worst environment for studying. (You might fall asleep!)

Make sure your study area is quiet, well-lit, and at the correct room temperature for you. If you study at home, reserving a corner specially for studying (no matter how small) is a good idea. This encourages discipline and helps you to stay focused on studying while you're sitting in this special "corner."

SCHEDULE STUDY TIME

Study time is sacred. Don't put off studying till after you've watched all your favorite TV shows. Study, *then* treat yourself to your favorite shows. Make studying the first thing on your list. It's school first, everything else second. Even though you should balance LIVING with being a law student, studying should be your priority. Because when you're a law student, falling behind in your studying and reading can be fatal. You'll always think you can catch up, but you know what? Most times, you never do. And, of course, cramming at the last minute is against the rules. So keep up with your studies. Life is a lot less complicated when you keep up, rather than having to play catch-up.

FORM STUDY GROUPS

Study groups are like knapsacks. They work for some, they don't work for others. If you're one of those people who works best with company, a study group might be right for you.

The aim is to get up to four people together to brainstorm after class at least a couple of times per week during the semester. Pick people you feel you can work with—not necessarily your best friend or the most "fun" people.

A study group helps in that one person may pick up on something that the others miss and vice versa. By sharing and exchanging, you all become more enriched. In addition, study groups serve as wonderful support groups. There is nothing more alienating than trying to get through law school with no one to sit and talk with.

Beware: During the week of finals, only meet with your study group after you've spent quality time alone, stuffing the material into your brain. The act of writing your exam is a solo venture. *You* have to know your stuff for yourself. So after you've gotten comfortable with working alone for a few days (right before the actual exam), then, meet with your group for one final brainstorm.

SEEK HELP

Never be too proud to admit you need help. Pride feels no pain! In addition to joining a study group, there are other places you can go for help if you feel overwhelmed. For example, most schools have academic-support programs to help students who are having a hard time making the transition to law school. More than likely, an upperclass person who has taken classes with the same professors you now have and who has been through what you're going through will be your mentor. They can advise you on everything from how to develop good study skills, to what outlines to buy. Make use of these helpful resources.

MONITOR PHONE TIME

If you study at home, this time should be uninterrupted, with the phone off limits. Unless it's a dire emergency, let your machine pick up when the phone rings. You can always return a call later.

There are many technological advances—like answering services and caller I.D. that make it a lot easier to screen calls. If you're not disciplined enough to let the machine pick up or if you can't afford an answering service, unplug the phone altogether or turn the phone off so you can't hear it ringing during your study time. Be disciplined. After a while, your family and friends will learn your phone schedule and they'll realize that if they call you before a certain time you won't answer.

AVOID PHONE PROBLEMS

To avoid the phone problem altogether, buy an answering machine if you don't have one. That way you won't miss important calls. Then, leave the cell phone at home and study in your school's library or in a public library. Of course, there are other problems you'll have to face—either you'll encounter inconsiderate people who won't shut up long enough for you to concentrate (wear ear-plugs), or fellow classmates will keep stopping by to chitchat (find secluded places to hide). But when all is said and done, choose the lesser of all the evils—study at home and be bothered by constant telephone interruptions, or, to get away from the phone altogether, study in the library and be bothered by classmates. If you choose home, remember: Phone is off limits!

UNDERSTAND THE
DIFFERENCE BETWEEN QUANTITY
AND QUALITY OF STUDY TIME

You'll try to convince yourself that everything is more important than studying. The gamut runs from eating to running to the drugstore for dental floss. Don't let your errant mind control you. Develop a study plan and stick to it, no matter what.

It is worth keeping in mind that quality study time, not quantity of time spent studying, is what counts. Be sure you understand this crucial difference. The difference is that those who study the longest don't necessarily get the best grades. They just go crazier. The idea is to understand what you are reading. Did you get the gist of what the Court said? Can you apply what the Court said to a hypothetical situation? If you can answer these questions, you'll know if your study sessions are qualitatively correct. (See Rule 56.)

TAPE-RECORD YOUR CLASSES

Taping is an incredibly effective study device. You literally have access to every single lecture right at your fingertips, so that if you missed what the professor said in class or you didn't understand your notes, you can listen to the tape over and over again until you do understand. (It's amazing what you miss by just taking notes in class or sitting there petrified, hoping your professor won't call on you!) You don't have to record all of your classes. Record only the ones that are giving you trouble. And don't erase your tapes till the end of the semester. You never know when you'll need to review a particular class. Then recycle the tapes for new classes in future semesters.

Be Aware of the Dangers of Tape-Recording

Be warned: You have to be very disciplined when recording your classes. Don't let the tapes pile up for months or even weeks before you listen to them. Most important, don't stop taking notes in class because you're recording it! In fact, if you find that you've stopped taking notes and have stopped paying attention because of the security you think you're getting from recording, shelve your tape recorder immediately. You may not be able to listen to all the tapes you allowed to pile up during the semester. Furthermore, if you didn't take class notes, didn't pay attention, and on top of that you didn't read for class—all because you were taping—you, my friend, are a carcass.

Buy a Computer

You need a computer. So consider investing in a laptop if you have an extra $1,500 or so to spend. The sheer convenience and portability makes a laptop a good idea. But if you don't have a computer and would feel more comfortable with a desktop, then get that. Whatever you decide to get—desktop or laptop—you need a computer in law school.

Being without a computer in law school is like jogging in dress shoes. It can be done, but why make law school more hellish than necessary? Who wants to be running around like a chicken without a head looking for a computer the morning your first legal writing assignment (worth a big chunk of the final grade, mind you) is due? All the other "computerless" people are going to be there competing for the computers! And on top of that, almost all the printers are going to be jammed, or, worst-case scenario, the computer will have a virus and it will eat your work. And you know what? You won't have a hard copy to back it up.

Sound farfetched? Don't be too blasé. Things happen in law school. So get a computer. Importantly, if you do get a laptop you might want to insure it for theft or loss. (See the General References appendix for more information.)

Appreciate the Perks of Owning a Computer

In addition to all the perks of having WordPerfect and Microsoft Word at your finger-tips, think of how convenient it would be to have Lexis and Westlaw (legal-research software you can download on your home computer so you can do your research at home) just a CD-ROM away. Still not sold on the idea of getting a computer? How about being able to get on the Internet at any hour of the day or night to hear the latest sports news and weather? Or, if you get a laptop, imagine being able to type your notes in class as the professor is lecturing? The latter cuts down on the time you will spend actually writing an outline, especially if you're one of those people who don't use the actual "typing of your outline" to "study." One caveat: If you hit the keys too hard the noise might annoy your classmates. So be considerate.

BRIEF YOUR CASES

Briefing is a must throughout the entire first year of law school. In fact the argument can be made that it is a must throughout law school, but you certainly don't want to make the mistake of thinking you can get by without briefing in 1L.

What is a brief? Good question. A brief is a kind of "brief" summary or synopsis of a case. It shouldn't be longer than a page. Basically, you summarize a case from the casebook as you read it, using the IRAC or CRA method. (See Rule 44.)

Brief as you go along. Because if you don't, you may regret it come exam time. You won't remember what the cases were about, so you won't be able to synthesize them. You'll have to reread the cases to some extent when you do your outline because your incomprehensible notes in the margins won't help you. This is a big waste of time.

Your peers might try to talk you out of briefing, especially if they aren't doing it. Don't listen to them. Keep briefing and leave a blank page after each brief so that you can write down your professor's take on the case during the lecture. Come time to outline, you'll be glad you did. Oh, and highlight key points as you read and/or write. That way, when it's time to brief, the key points of the case will jump right out at you!

Know What IRAC
and CRA Mean

When briefing and writing a law school exam, remember that the IRAC method (1) spots the **ISSUE** in a case. What is the issue? The issue is the legal question or questions you're about to answer.

Next, you must (2) identify the **RULE** of law. What is the rule? The rule is the statement of law relevant to the facts.

Then you (3) **APPLY** the rule to the given facts to the facts of the case. How does the court decide? That's the conclusion. So you (4) state a **CONCLUSION,** based on all of the above.

The CRA method does much of the same. It's the sequence that's different. It starts with (1) the **CONCLUSION,** then states (2) the **RULE,** then (3) **APPLIES** the rule to the facts.

KEY IN ON LECTURES

Keying in on lectures is paramount. Attend all lectures unless there's a dire emergency. It's the only way to hear the professor's "magic words," which you need to throw back on your exam booklet if you want a decent grade. (See Rule 38.)

By the second year of law school, you can afford to think (if you choose) that going to class, or keying in on lectures, is a complete waste of time; but not in the first year. You don't know what you're doing yet. Pay strict attention to the lecture. Take notes, record your classes and participate in class discussions whenever you're able.

USE COMMERCIAL AIDS

For some 1Ls, commercial aids are dirty little secrets. Most would rather die than admit they use them. But rest assured that almost everybody uses them—at least by the second semester of their law school career when they learn the secret. Those who use commercial aids will dazzle and baffle you. They'll make you feel stupid at worst, or a slow learner at best—particularly if you don't yet know they're using. Don't be fooled any longer. Get yours! (Definitely get Emanuel for Civil Procedure and Gilberts for Property. And Casenote Legal Briefs are essential.)

Commercial aids users often get better grades because, for one thing, they get credit for spitting the stuff they get from these aids at their professors. And remember this: Once users get an edge on you this early in the game (grade-wise), it's very hard to catch up with them. And no, this isn't about competing with anybody. It's about improving your grade if you can and doing the very best for yourself.

DON'T LISTEN TO PROFESSORS WHO TELL YOU NOT TO USE COMMERCIAL AIDS

Most law students agree that commercial aids are great supplements to any professor's lectures because they put the course in perspective, direct you in approaching questions on the exam, and outline the material in a comprehensive way.

However, some professors abhor them and will tell you not to use them. My advice is: Don't listen! And I say that respectfully. Commercial tapes and outlines, when used correctly, can make the difference between an embarrassing grade and one you can actually discuss with your buddies. The professor's lectures alone are not always enough because sometimes it's hard to see the connections you're supposed to make. (Besides, notice that the professors who hate outlines the most are usually the worst at teaching the material!)

The rule is: Use aids constructively. That means that you must also take good class notes so that you can remember your professor's "magic words" and use them on your exam (never underestimate the power of those "magic words!"). But wise up to the benefits of commercial aids. They help.

DON'T DEPEND SOLELY ON COMMERCIAL AIDS

It's folly to depend solely on commercial aids. Aids are supplements, *not* substitutes. No commercial aid is a substitute for your professor's notes and reading the casebook. Never, ever, lose sight of this pivotal truth! Still, if you decide to "use," don't wait till the end of the semester or when finals are two days away. Use them throughout the semester. They can help you to be brave. You'll start raising your hand in class and baffling the poor, unsuspecting students who don't know your dirty little secret.

WRITE YOUR OWN OUTLINE

One of the things you need to get a head start on during the semester is writing your own outline for your final exam. What is meant by write your own outline? It is simply another way of saying you should "arrange your notes into a logical fashion so that you can begin to study for the final." If your school offers any seminars on how to write a good outline (and most schools do), please attend. What you learn will be invaluable. You can also find sample outlines on the Web. (See Rule 51.)

Popular consensus among fellow students seems to be that the sooner you start outlining for your final exam, the better. You should have definitely started your outline for each class four weeks before the final—at the very latest. Otherwise, you'll be faced with an almost insurmountable amount of work at the last minute and then the whole purpose of doing your own outline (namely, drilling the material into your brain) will be defeated because you'll be typing frantically just to get to the end—and retaining absolutely nothing.

The point of writing your own outline is not unlike that of using the commercial ones; it's to get the best grade you can on your final. When you do your own outline, it's seeping into your head as you type or write. That's why it's better to do an outline of your own, even if you are getting one from an upperclass person or the Internet. You don't want to get into the final exam with the best outline an upperclass person gave you, but with no idea of where to find anything and no clue as to the Black-Letter Law (Black-Letter Law is defined in *Blacks Law Dictionary* as "the basic principles of law generally accepted by the courts") and the emerging trends covered in class.

STRUCTURE YOUR OUTLINE

The rule is to structure the outline in a way that makes sense to you and is unique to the way your professor covered the material in class. You'll need your syllabus and class notes, or textbooks for this. Remember those briefs you kept up with all semester? (See Rule 43.) Well, they'll come in really handy now. If you did a thorough job with summarizing the cases, you won't have to use your textbook at all. By using the syllabus and briefs, you can create your outline.

Exactly how do you go about outlining? There are many ways. The easiest and best way is to dump all the facts of the case into the garbage (after you've reviewed them) and suck out the rule of law. Sometimes that's just one sentence. Example: "minimum contacts equals fair play and substantial justice." (Note: doing your outline this way will only make sense to you if you understood the context in which the court used the rule in the first place.)

If this is how you choose to do your outline, it will probably amount to ten pages or so. This is good. A ten-page outline might be a lot more useful to you than the ridiculously long fifty-page outlines that a lot of students take into exams.

Another way to structure your outline is to summarize each

brief. (In other words, write a "brief" brief.) Then synthesize each brief: That is, find the legal connection between the different cases and determine the rule of law for each. (Sometimes it's helpful to include in your outline the respective jurisdiction of the case. That way, you can indicate to your professor on the exam that, though a particular interpretation is the majority view, there is an emerging minority trend as well.) However, *how* you choose to do your outline is entirely up to you. Believe it or not, some law students don't do outlines at all, but simply go over their notes several times. So do your outline in the way that works best for you.

Surf the Internet for Sample Exams and Outlines

There are a couple of creative ways to get sample exams and outlines. First, most professors have old exams and sample answers on file in the library. It's a good idea to get hold of your professor's exams as early in the semester as you can.

As the professor covers a particular topic, answer that portion of the exam. Once you've written out your answer to this sample question, have your professor critique it. What better way to know how your professor wants the exam written? Doing the "old exam" bit is singularly the best thing you can do if you want a good grade on your final. Many professors ask the same exact questions every single year! They just word the questions differently.

Second, professors who teach the same subject (in your school or in another) tend to ask similar exam questions. Bet you didn't know that sample exams of some of these professors can be found on the Web. So browse the Internet and see what's out there. Ditto for outlines. Try www.findlaw.com. It's chock full of good stuff that can help you. *The New York Law Journal* also has a section on their website just for law students. You can find that at www.nylj.com.

TRY NOT TO USE
SOMEONE ELSE'S OUTLINE

There is a serious problem in using someone else's outline on a law school exam. You see, time is the enemy on a law school exam. It flies like you wouldn't believe—especially if you aren't familiar with the outline you're using. Even though many exams will be open book, you won't have time to be searching through fifty pages of somebody else's outline if you don't know exactly where things are. So keep that in mind if you decide not to write your own outline. If you decide to use someone else's outline, thoroughly familiarize yourself with it so as to waste less time "fishing" during the exam.

Use "Magic Words"
to Get "Brownies"

Your grade in law school depends on the amount of points you rack up. "Brownie points" is a term I use to refer to these points. Obviously, the more brownies you get, the higher your grade will be. Everybody loves and wants brownies. Knowing how to maximize these brownies is not always easy. The following list is hardly exhaustive but it might help to maximize your brownies on a given exam.

Know what your professors want. Yes, that's right. You've got to learn to read your professors' minds.

You'll have to be good at spotting issues, and you have to be good at legal analysis. Get all the study guides that help you perfect these skills.

IRAC, IRAC, IRAC. Keep in mind that you want to be IRAC-ing the right issue. If you have the best analysis in the world, but the wrong issue analyzed, you've got a problem.

Use your professor's "magic" words. Don't get creative. They don't care that you have a brain and you can put things in your own words, so leave the creativity for your novel. Spit the stuff back to them exactly how they said it in class. (You'll know the magic words only if you've been going to class!) And argue both sides of the issue.

Watch your handwriting. One professor I know admitted to being turned off by sloppy, illegible handwriting. He announced to the class that he usually grades exams based on an initial "feel" he gets upon first glance of the paper. Can you imagine?! So try to write as neatly as you can. Yes, you have serious time constraints on a law school exam, and penmanship is the last thing on your mind, but for all too many law students, a sloppy, messy paper can cost you dearly! Your professor could just tune out and give you a D. Frightening, but true. So, if you know your handwriting is atrocious, perhaps you should arrange to type your final. Many schools give this option.

Finally, the night before your final, make sure you get a lot of sleep so that your brain will be in tiptop shape. And once you get your exam, take a deep breath before you begin.

DO A PRE-ANSWER

Many law professors ask the same question every year. They just word it differently. Do you know what that means? You can actually pre-write the answer to many of your exams! This has got to be the biggest secret in law school. By the time many law students figure it out, it's already third year and they've already gotten a truckload of horrendous grades!

For this pre-answer idea to work, first you have to go through the professor's old exams. Get a feel for how this professor thinks. Look for a pattern in the questions. Get into this person's head. Then do a generic answer that can be adapted to almost any question. Make sure you have all the "magic words" and phrases from this professor's mouth, and from the text.

Don't have a typed, six-page, single-spaced, pre-answer to your two-hour contracts exam. Remember that time is of the essence on a law school exam. Oh, and time yourself when you're practicing writing these pre-answers using the same time that is allotted for the exam. Practice, practice, practice. This will make a big difference in your grade.

No Cramming!

Don't dream for one moment that you can slack off and cram an entire semester of law school into one night of studying—the night before the final. In this respect, law school is very different from college. You can't cram. Unless, of course, you want your brain to spill out your ears.

You have to prepare for exams in increments along the way. It's easier to study in small chunks instead of big ones, particularly if you have a short attention span. In fact, you might find that studying in blocks of three hours at a time—say from 6 P.M. to 9 P.M. every night—is the best strategy. Everybody is different so if you can study for eight hours at a time, do what's best for you! Just know from the outset that you can't cram three months of work into one night of frantic studying. Especially not in 1L. Keep up with your reading. Study a little every day. It works.

Don't Overstudy

There's a bizarre phenomenon called *overstudying*. This is just as fatal as not studying at all. Talk about hell.

What's important when preparing for exams is not so much going over everything for weeks and weeks on end and memorizing every word of the text, but to understand what your professor wants and systematize the material in such a way that it (1) makes sense to you and (2) reflects what your professor said he's looking for.

Overstudying isn't the key to success. Often, it is the key to failure. Knowing how to write a well-organized, analyzed response the way your professor *wants* you to write it is the key. Studying till your face hurts so much you can't wear your glasses and being able to spit out the material in three languages isn't usually the key. On top of that, what gets you an A with your Contracts professor isn't necessarily what gets you an A with your Torts professor. The better you are at anticipating your individual professor's questions, the more qualitatively correct your study sessions will be, and the better your grade will probably be. Again, it's not about overstudying. It's about anticipation, analysis, and organization. (See Rule 38.)

DON'T AGONIZE OVER
ATROCIOUS GRADES

When you get your grades and they are not what you expected, the first thing to do is immediately see your professor and find out where you went wrong. Don't wait till you've had three consecutive years of getting horrendous grades to try to assess the problem. Yes, it's better late than never, but try to nip the problem in the bud—as early as you can. Chances are you could be making simple mistakes—such as the way you organized your answer—which, if left unfixed, could mess you up on future exams, including the Bar!

Next, keep a few things in mind: for example, the grading in law school is highly subjective. It is subject to the whims of each professor. Each professor has a completely different dynamic. Frankly, sometimes what they're looking for is but a complete conundrum . . . In fact, if you didn't know better you could almost swear that after writing what you know in your heart is an A paper, your professor sits back in his jacuzzi, Scotch in hand and smoking a cigar after eating an entire roast by himself and goes: "Hmm . . . C!!!" without reading a single word you wrote. And then when you go to the registrar (after getting over the initial shock) to try to convince somebody that the man suffers from severe dementia at best, they threaten to call security on you if you don't leave the premises at once. Well, some things are just outside your locus of control. So as long as it's not an F, you're probably better off forgetting about it and moving on.

Next, remember that taking a law school exam is an art, and you and your classmates are the artists. How many Michelangelos and Piccassos do you know, after all? But remember that one person's Piccasso is another person's "What-the-heck-is-this!" So just because your professor didn't like what you wrote in your blue book doesn't mean it wasn't pretty darned good.

Also, remember that some people just "test" better than others. That is, it's not that they're smarter. They just test better. Unlike you, they may thrive in high-pressure situations—like taking law school exams—where they have ONE SHOT to organize, analyze, think, write, and show their professor that they know the material. You might want to consider taking a lot of paper courses if you're prone to panic on exams once you get to 2L and 3L. In the meantime, keep in mind that in the real world, you'll have a lot more than three hours to prepare your case or what-have-you. So don't think that the fact that you don't perform well on law school exams means you won't perform well as an attorney, or that you're not smart. It could also just be that under the totality of circumstances that were present at the time you took the exam, those who "tested" better wanted the "A" a little more than you did.

The bottom-line is, don't sweat your grades. As long as they're not D's and F's, chances are you'll still graduate; and you don't get to wear your grades on your lapels when you leave law school. An upperclass person once said: You don't have to get great grades to become a lawyer. But you do have to graduate. Now, who was it who said, "The race is not for the swift but for those who endure to the end"?

The "Grading" Rule

Most, if not all, law schools grade anonymously and are very strict about preserving the integrity of this policy. This is a good policy. It's the best known way to ensure *some* semblance of fairness with grading.

So this rule is: Even if you're best buddies with your professor and you play golf with him and Tiger Woods every single weekend, this won't (or shouldn't) affect your grade. If it does, you *and* your professor could wind up with disciplinary charges, up to and including being thrown out of law school.

Of course, if you were to be discharged from your school for something like this, it would be difficult if not impossible to get into another. So watch out.

4

PROFESSORS

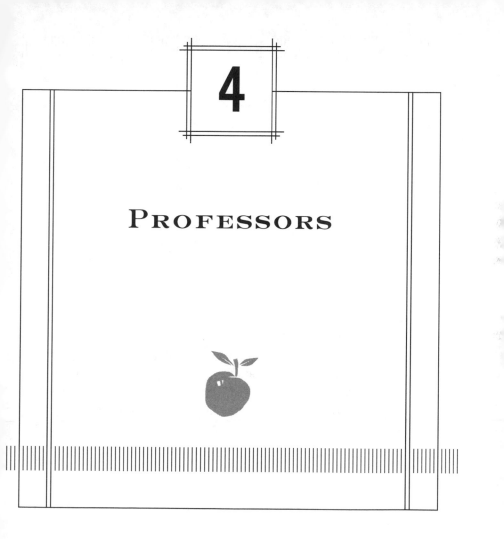

GET TO KNOW AT LEAST ONE PROFESSOR

Get to know at least one professor on a one-on-one basis. It's not feasible to do this right after class when twenty other students are trying to do exactly the same thing. Not to worry. Most professors schedule office hours and most are eager to sit and chat with students. Take the time to schedule a visit—whether you have a question about a concept you didn't quite grasp, or simply want to give praise on the handling of particular subject matter in class, or to ask questions in general about the legal field, or whatever.

A good reason to get acquainted with your professor is so that you have a reference when you're applying for a job. If you went straight to law school from college, you might not have any choice but to get a good reference from a professor since you won't have job or life experience to draw on.

DON'T FALL IN LOVE
WITH YOUR PROFESSOR

Never get romantically involved with someone who has the power to give you an A or a D+ on your exam. Yes, some law professors are lethally attractive, highly distinguished, unbelievably intelligent, and utterly powerful. Yes, their eyes twinkle seductively when they smile. Yes, their tummies are flat. Yes, you're in awe of them. Yes, you just want to eat them up. But don't!

First, most of them are married. Second, getting involved romantically with someone who has that much authority over you is always going to be sticky and tricky. Such a relationship is simply not conducive to a healthy academic rapport.

Oh, and even if your professor is single, his or her belly is not *that* flat, you're absolutely positive you'll never take his or her class, and you're so in love it hurts, still you shouldn't get involved. It just wouldn't look right. And remember Murphy's Law?! (Think Bill Clinton and Monica Lewinsky!) Above all, avoid the very appearance of impropriety.

Now, does this mean you can't have sinfully, deliciously, wickedly impure thoughts about this professor? Of course not! But, go no further!!!

Accept that All Your Professors May Not Like You

Let's say you find yourself in a situation where you like a professor and want this professor to be your mentor. You visit during office hours and try to establish rapport. But in spite of being "honey sweet," your professor just doesn't like your face, your hair, your style of dress, or YOU.

What to do? Don't take it personally or to heart. Perhaps your professor is just really busy and you have really bad timing. Or maybe you remind your professor of her old boyfriend; or you remind him of someone who used to beat him up when he was in junior high. Better yet, maybe you're just visiting too much. Stop. Back off. Keep in mind that not everybody will like you just because you like them. Accept. Move on. Find another professor to admire, one who will be happy to be your mentor.

RESPECT GOOD PROFESSORS

Normally, you'll find that only one or two professors in your entire law school career inspire you. They have the ability—just by breathing, perhaps—to make you feel excited about learning the law. This is the mark of a good professor.

A "good professor" is a purely subjective thing. What's good to you may be horrible to someone else. That's fine. You're allowed to like who you choose, and so are they. You'll probably look upon a good professor with the utmost reverence for the rest of your life. You may even find yourself sitting in his office gushing, "You're my favorite professor!"

The rule to remember is: Don't be too openly adoring. Don't call too often or show up at this professor's office every day. If you're thought of as a pest, or worse, that wouldn't be good.

LEARN TO SPOT THE BAD
PROFESSORS: TYPE I

The first type of bad professors are those who are just bad teachers. They're brilliant, but not good at teaching. You'll probably have at least one professor like this. This means you'll end up teaching yourself the entire course with a professor like this. This is the rule: Get a commercial outline. You'll need it. The good news is that having to teach yourself is not such a bad thing. The extra effort you make means the material will stick in your mind for a long time. So look on the bright side!

Learn to Spot the Bad Professors: Type II

There's another type of "bad" professor that you want to watch out for. These are just bad people. These professors try to take advantage of their superior position. They'll try to sock it to you one way or another if they don't like you for whatever reason or sense you don't like them. They get off on making you feel like crap—and that's probably the only thing they're good at. They may even openly despise you and the law and all the justices who ever sat on the bench and life itself. Going to their class is about as much fun as the prospect of colon surgery. What to do? Not much you can do. Hopefully you won't get a professor like this in the first place, but if you do, forget about getting the professor fired. Chances are he or she is "tenured." So you'll be wasting your time and making a bad name for yourself in the law school community—especially if this professor is popular with other students but has a personal beef with you! This is the rule: Know when you're outmatched. Behave accordingly. It sure makes law school life a whole lot easier. (But see Rule 66.)

Recognize Sexual Harassment

It's improbable that you'll be sexually harassed in law school. Most law professors and law school personnel know the law, respect it, and are unlikely to sexually harass a litigious law student. In fact, you're probably more likely to be the one trying to get their attention than they are to pick you out from among hundreds of students. But stranger things have happened. Look at the allegations against Justice Clarence Thomas and President Bill Clinton! (I should point out that none of these accusations have been proven.)

What, exactly, is sexual harassment? It's basically a power trip where somebody uses their position of power to force somebody else into an *unwelcome* sexual situation, or subject that person to a hostile work or educational environment.

Sexual harassment has more to do with an abuse of power than sexual desire (although you might argue that one has everything to do with the other). This misconduct seems akin to emotional "rape," more than anything else, in that the victims often feel emotionally violated and assaulted.

Because sexual harassment has become such a hot issue (there are even cases of men harassing other men and women harassing men), many companies, schools, and organizations have instituted policies to protect against it. Law schools are no exception.

So this is the rule: If, by some chance, this happens to you, assert yourself from the beginning. Let the harasser know that you know your rights and you won't tolerate his/her violation of those rights. Then you may want to confide in someone you trust. Tell them what's been going on. If not, get a copy of your school's guidelines from the registrar. It will tell you exactly how to file a complaint.

Also, be aware that many communities have sexual harassment workshops geared toward arming victims of sexual harassment with preventive techniques, awareness of options, and possible solutions. Remember, if you are a victim of sexual harassment, it is not your fault. You don't have to take it.

ZIP YOUR LIPS

Don't bad-mouth a professor, members of your law school's administration and staff, or anyone else, around people you do not know—especially if your school community is very small. This is totally against the rules.

A poet once said, "Even blades of grass are living ears." In other words, people are listening when you least suspect that they are. They may take back your words and comments to the person you were bad-mouthing. They may even misquote you or exaggerate what you said and before you know it, you'll have a really bad name. (And don't think people don't know who you are. Remember your photo ID from first year? It's on file and you can be identified quite easily by people you don't know.)

Bad-mouthing a professor is the worst of all. If you bad-mouth a professor and this professor hears about it (you never know how news gets around but it does), they have the power to completely demolish you in class in front of your peers, standing behind the protective confines of that lectern. And even assuming your school's grading is anonymous, you can bet that anonymity can be decoded and your professor can get back at you.

Does that mean you should put up with abuse from a professor? Of course not. If you really feel in your heart that a professor has crossed the line in some way, tell someone you trust—maybe another professor, a friend, or whoever. Or confront the professor privately to put them on "notice" that you felt infringed upon.

If the professor's conduct continues, you might want to think about filing an official complaint at your school's Office of Student Affairs. But this is a big move that can immerse you in a bureaucratic mess. So think things through carefully before you take this step. Most of the time, you won't have to take this course or action.

But there will be times when it's the only course to take. You'll have to decide. The idea is you want to assure yourself that if your professor (or whoever) has a personal vendetta against you and the situation arises where you have to defend yourself in a hearing (for example, the professor gave you an F in the class), you want to make sure there is a "bureaucratic paper trail" to which you can refer.

So the general rules are: If you can't say something neutral, zip your lips. Don't bad-mouth anybody. Then, always consider the gravity of the harm before you take action. In other words, to whom are you complaining? And how important is whatever it is that you're complaining about in the grand scheme of things? Can it wait till you get home and let off steam with your mom? If yes, do that. If not, consider the other alternatives suggested. What you shouldn't do is go around complaining to everybody. They probably can do nothing but make things worse by spreading gossip. That wouldn't be best for you at all.

Oh, and resist the urge to spill your entire guts—all your hopes, dreams, sins, desires, and aspirations—to your fellow classmates (or anybody else for that matter) till you get to know them fairly well. (First-years tend to go a bit overboard in this respect, spilling all their secrets to people they barely know. Maybe they're just nervous. Or they feel an overwhelming sense of camaraderie because they're sharing an unusually intense experience with these strangers.) But no matter how well you think you've come to know your classmates after the first few weeks of school, you really don't know them well enough to spill your guts. Wait till 2L, at least, to decide who your friends really are before you tell all about yourself. Otherwise it may come back to haunt you. Again, zip your lips shut!

5

DO'S AND DON'TS

Get a Weekly Planner

Be organized; period, end of story. Organization is one of the most important criteria for a successful law school career. You'll have a lot to do. If you're not careful, you'll miss important deadlines—like your midterm. Can you imagine the horror?

So get yourself a weekly planner/scheduler. This planner can be an academic wall calendar, Palm Pilot, or Sharp Wizard Organizer (these are a bit pricier). If you don't have that much money to spend, buy the academic wall calendar from any stationary store for about $10.00. It's worth the investment. Hang it in your room, on your fridge, or some place where you'll see it at all times.

Jot down every single thing you have to do—including studying, going to the movies, doctors' appointments, meetings for clubs or panel discussions, making whoopie.

Prioritize. Allot a time limit for everything; that is, write down a cut-off point for each goal. Stop at the allotted time, no matter what. Tick things off your list as you accomplish them (this will make you feel like you're getting somewhere). Finally, designate a time to stop completely for the day (for example, 11:00 P.M.). After a time, you'll develop a routine and your life is guaranteed to be a lot easier.

SET REALISTIC GOALS

Make sure your goals are realistic. You'll be more likely to stick to them. Only you know your capabilities and limits. Keep your limits in mind when you go about planning your day, week, or semester, because setting unrealistic goals will frustrate you—and you surely don't need any extra frustrations in law school.

Remember: There are only twenty-four hours in a day. You're only one human being. Don't schedule twelve hours of study per day when you know that you're only productive for half that time. Don't sabotage yourself. Don't add to your problems. Always do what's best for you, and what's best for you can never be "unrealistic" for you.

SIGN UP EARLY FOR A
BAR REVIEW COURSE

It's never too early to start thinking about the bar exam. Taking the bar exam is the final assault you'll endure before they let you call yourself an attorney. Plan for it as early as in the first year of law school. It will make your life less hellish three years down the road.

Lurking somewhere around your school (almost from the first day of law school) are bound to be sales reps from different bar review courses who will wine, dine, and pamper you with course outlines; tips on writing exams; promises of "passing the bar on the first shot, or a free repeat course if you don't"; free candy, pens, highlighters, and myriad other goodies. But you have to sign up with their course to get the whopping discount three years down the road. Seriously consider their offers. Luxuriate in their freebies and attention.

There are excellent reasons for signing up early for a bar review course. When you sign up in the first year of law school (as opposed to later in your law school career), you'll be able to "lock in" the price of the course, thus save yourself a bundle (hundreds of dollars) three years down the road. And the best part is, except for a membership fee, you don't have to cough up the money till the last semester of your third year of law school.

Also, you will receive free outlines for every course. You'll also be able to attend live lectures for courses you need extra help with. You may even qualify for one of the bar review scholarships if you meet certain criteria (anywhere from $100 off to a full scholarship if you become a sales rep) and thus avoid having to pay the astronomical price of the course that is charged to those less "industrious" than yourself.

Signing up early for a bar review course has other fringe benefits. For one thing you'll have to start thinking about taking the Multi-State Professional Responsibility Exam (MPRE—otherwise known as the Ethics part of the bar exam) long before you graduate. This exam is not given at the same time as the rest of the bar exam. Just about every law student has to take this exam and you might want to inquire about it at the registrar. Bar review courses offer their members free prep courses and outlines for the MPRE! So this is another good reason to sign up early.

Only Compete with Yourself

Break the competitive mold that pits law students against each other. This might actually make your law school experience more rewarding. Yes, there can be such a thing as a non-competitive law student. And they are probably "happier" than all their competitive peers combined.

This is not to say that competition is bad, though. Quite the contrary. You know competition is generally cost-efficient. Competition produces better attorneys in the "marketplace." And consumers will benefit by having smarter, sharper attorneys. And yes, the law student who is trying to out-do classmates (or competing!) might study harder and longer in an effort to come out on top . . .

But maybe not. The weird thing about law school is that studying longer and harder (see Rules 38 and 56) doesn't necessarily mean you'll get better grades. You'll probably just be the first to burn out. So why try to keep up with the Joneses in the first place? Let the Joneses get an aneurysm (actually that's not very "nice," is it?), if they so choose! Instead of competing with the Joneses, be content with your very best. After all, contentment, not competition, is the secret to youthful good looks and marvelous clear skin.

If, of course, you decide that the thrill is in the competing, does it have to be dog-eat-dog? Your aim should not be to sabotage your peers by tearing pages from books you know they will need; or telling your clinic teammate that an important interview with a client is 2:00 P.M. when you know full well the interview is really 1:00 P.M. and that showing up late will make your teammate look really bad; or committing other unsaintly deeds. Instead, try to make the experience easier for your peers in whatever small way you can. Because whatever you dish out in this life always comes back to you, tenfold—if not in law school, then when you get out in the world. And if not then, you'll surely get yours in your next life. So watch out.

Know Upperclass People

Speaking of upperclass people: Get to know them. There's a tendency for students to hang out with other students from their section, or year, almost exclusively. That might be a mistake. It's imperative that you get to know other students, especially upperclass students.

Upperclass students are an endless source of information. By 2L, all law students become veterans of the law school game, having fallen into one or the other law school pit. They could all write the book on how to survive and, as such, can help you.

Upperclass people can direct and advise you in ways that other first-years, who are in the same boat as you, can't. And for obvious reasons. Upperclass people have been there, done that. Other first-years have not. Usually these students are only too glad to offer any help they can. So all you have to do is ask for help. Keep an open mind and be friendly to everyone.

JOIN CLUBS

Your legal education continues outside the classroom. If you wish, and time permits, there are many clubs you can participate in. Clubs can enhance your appreciation for the law and how it works, while at the same time offer a reprieve from the grind of studying. Variety is the idea here. You want to get a feel for a variety of areas of the law. Why not join a club like the National Lawyers' Guild or the International Law Society? Many clubs meet about four times in the whole semester and all you have to do is show up and sign your name on a piece of paper and you have something new to put on your resume.

A club also presents a great opportunity to meet people from other first-year sections, as well as upperclass people. Try to join a club that interests you. Don't just sign up so that you'll have something to put on your resume. Sign up because you want to learn about that particular area of the law, because you want to enrich your law school experience, and because you want to interact with others in a fun, noncompetitive way. Most schools have at least ten different clubs, usually a lot more than that. So, if you're willing to widen your horizons, the sky is the limit.

ATTEND LUNCHEONS AND PANELS

Attend as many functions such as luncheons and panel discussions as you can. (Maybe one or two per semester is realistic.) These are hosted by law firms, bar associations, and other associations such as the legal aid societies. And there is no fee. In addition to the exotic appetizers they're bound to serve, you will probably pick up valuable bits of information that makes the difference in your legal education and career.

These events are likely to present great networking opportunities—especially if you're past your first year of law school. You're bound to meet many interesting attorneys and judges and other business people. If you hit it off with one of these people, you could even volunteer your time in the summer or get a flat-out job offer after graduation! Have some business cards made up so that you can distribute them to prospective contacts. They'll be impressed.

Be Assertive and Meet "The One"

Some people meet their future spouses in law school. What better place to meet a highly accomplished, intelligent person who shares your interests? Many professors have even met their spouse in law school. So there is, apparently, romance among those dusty, old law books, and you might be one of the lucky ones who meet your future significant other there. But only if you don't play that shy game and lose the woman/man of your dreams. You've got to be assertive! Sometimes it's the only way to get what you want.

If you like someone, give some indication of your feelings. If you're a nervous wreck when you meet unexpectedly, take deep breaths. Count to ten, slowly. Do anything that you know will calm you down (except pass out). You'll need these very techniques sometime in your career anyway, so the time to practice is now.

Choose "the one" wisely, of course. Make sure this person is not a louse before you get heavily involved and that all of your feelings are reciprocated. Unfortunately, just because you like someone doesn't mean they'll ever like you as anything but a platonic friend. Yikes! (Yes, it hurts. But you'll live.

Just move on. Grin and bear it. You'll find your dream person eventually.)

Oh, and give "it" at least a few months before you make whoopie. And *please* practice safe sex! Do you really want to risk your physical and emotional well-being with someone you've known only a few weeks? Rushing into bad relationships is always a bad idea, but in law school it's academic disaster.

Don't Be a Loudmouth

Don't be a loudmouth. Law students tend not to like classmates who are loudmouths. What's a loudmouth? Someone (male or female) who always speaks in an overly loud, obnoxious, and aggressive fashion and comes off as a know-it-all. It's not what you say. It's not what you know. It's how you say what you know.

The rule is: Tone down your voice if you tend to speak loudly and aggressively. Be noncondescending. Don't shove your views down other people's throats. Spoon it to them intelligently, calmly, and modestly. They'll be more apt to hear you and like you.

6

HEALTH
AND COPING

GET MEDICAL INSURANCE

Good health is worth all the money, education, and riches this world has to offer. If you're lucky, your health is already good. But you must maintain it by seeing your physician at least once per year, and to do this, it's wise to get medical insurance. You just can't leave your health to chance (definitely get those flu shots!).

While taking care of your health is one of the most important undertakings for law students, it is often the most overlooked. Who has time to think about doctors and illness and maintaining health when you're trying to get through Contracts, Torts, Civil Procedure, and all the rest of it? The thing is, none of us is too young to get sick. The stresses of law school are enough to take their toll upon even Arnold Schwartznegger's resistance, never mind poor little you and me! But getting sick is an expensive commodity in law school. Especially when you're not covered by insurance.

You can buy insurance from major carriers at special student rates. Certain medical clinics offer special student rates for routine physicals and other services. Normally, all you have to do is show proof that you're a student and a financial statement from your bank in order to get the reduced rate. Check with local health clinics for further information.

Some dental schools also offer discounted dental service to students in the area. New York University's Kriser Dental Center in New York City, for example, offers such discounts. Usually you'll have to pay some sort of initial application fee, but thereafter you'll pay considerably less than full cost—sometimes up to 75% off for routine examinations and cleanings. So check with the local dental schools in your city to see if you qualify.

This is what you should do: Go to your Office of Student Affairs. See what's offered by your school. There are bound to be brochures that explain various insurance policies and how they work. (See the General References appendix for more information on some national policies.)

EAT WELL

Many law students literally live on the empty calories from chocolate bars and potato chips. It's the stress! But it's a bad bad idea. Do you want to become sluggish and fat? Of course not! You have to eat well when you're a law student. Fuel your body with nutritious food. Otherwise you won't be able to think straight, you'll become unraveled, and your life will be pure hell.

This doesn't imply you should diet. Never diet. Eat when you're hungry and stop eating when you're full. Eat a balanced meal. Snack in moderation. Exercise according to how much junk you eat if you don't want to put on twenty pounds. It's that simple.

FEED YOUR BRAIN

Food is energizing. The rule is: You can't have too much energy during law school. Natural energy, that is. Eating good food keeps your brain cells nourished and energized. As a result, handling the law school challenges will be a lot easier.

First of all you must eat lots of fruits and veggies. But you need more than fruits and veggies to be healthy. You need a balanced diet. Learn to prepare good foods that are healthy, quick, and easy. Let's talk about some of these good foods. For example, you need protein. How about this: Buy yourself a filet of salmon next time you go to the supermarket (salmon isn't cheap, but once per week won't break your bank account). Coat filet with parsley, unsalted whipped butter, a squeeze of lemon juice, and a whole jalapeno. Wrap in foil. Place in pre-heated 350° oven. Let steam gently for about fifteen minutes. Serve with a plateful of steamed veggies, nut bread, and a tall glass of water. This is healthy, quick, and easy! This recipe also works with a boneless chicken breast.

There are other sources of protein. Take pasta. It's a wonderful source of energy. Eat lots of it. It's filling. It's not fattening. It can take as little as seven minutes to prepare. Boil in salted water. Then serve with veggies and a can of tuna—or whatever. Another good protein source is pre-cooked Buffalo wings. Buy a week's supply of the frozen variety. Bake them all at once and store whatever you don't finish in the fridge. This can last you a whole week.

When pasta/protein gets boring, substitute with rice/carbohydrates. Buy "Minute Rice in a Bag," an incredible invention that takes four minutes to boil. Serve with steamed veggies and fish or Buffalo wings, or whatever you like.

A lot of Mediterranean dishes are quick fixes. Couscous is great. So is rice pilaf. You can prepare couscous in three minutes flat. It's a good source of iron (among other things), it's filling, and it tastes real good. Beans are a great source of iron too. So why not make a bean-toss salad! Open three different cans of beans—pinto, red, and chick peas. Mince onion and garlic, cut some scallions, squeeze a teaspoon of lemon juice and a tablespoon of olive oil. Toss everything together. Heat for five minutes. Serve with toast and red wine. And you thought you couldn't cook!

The point I'm trying to make is that eating good food is inexpensive and easy. And it can be quick too. Check out a cookbook or two or ask your parents about preparing simple meals. Or you can watch the cooking channel on TV. (You can also download the recipes from their website at www.foodtv.com.)

DRINK TONS OF WATER

Water is purifying and cleansing. Human beings need lots of it. Law students need even more. But when you're all caught up in the frenzy of law school, it's easy to forget to drink your eight glasses each day.

You can't forget. Drink tons of water. It's better than soda. It's better than beer. It's better than coffee. It's free. It'll clear your brain. It'll cleanse your body. It'll flush you out and make your skin look radiant and healthy. It'll get rid of that ashen, law school complexion. It'll make dry, cracked lips moist. (Get in the habit of drinking fresh water with a squeeze of lime or lemon. It's a great source of vitamin C!) And how cool will you look toting an Evian bottle every day? What more incentive do you need? Drink. And be merry.

Take Dietary Supplements

If you haven't been eating well and exercising, think about taking a daily multi-vitamin to supplement your diet. You probably know that a good dose of vitamin C helps to keep your immune system working efficiently. You'll get fewer colds and flus, thus miss fewer classes.

Vitamin E and aromatherapy (see Rule 108) are said to help memory. So that might be something you want to consider. Also, there's this herb called gingko-biloba that's also supposed to be really good for memory. So if you're into that kind of stuff, you might want to try it, but don't take too much of it. Studies show that excessive doses of gingko-biloba can affect fertility.

There are many other vitamins and minerals that could be beneficial to you. But keep in mind that too many vitamins can cause more harm than good. Some if taken in large doses can be toxic! So to be on the safe side, let your doctor recommend something for you.

SHAKE YOUR BOOTIE

Exercise is paramount. It relieves stress, clears the mind, and energizes the body. It'll make you feel stronger. It'll make you look so sexy, your classmates will be jealous when you come in struttin' your buff stuff! But don't gloat. Instead, offer to work out with them. Together, you can shake-shake-shake, shake-shake-shake, shake your collective booties. What could be more fun?

Ideally you should exercise regularly no matter what you're doing in your life. However, as a law school student, the benefits of a strong, healthy body and a clear, uncluttered mind, can never be overrated. The rule is to keep your body active when you're not in class or studying. (Of course, check with your doctor before starting any rigorous exercise program.)

Find the Time to Exercise!

Contrary to what you might think, you can make time for exercise if you really want to. As a matter of fact, you can find the time to do anything you truly want to do. If exercising and taking care of yourself are priorities in your life, you will find the time with almost no trouble. So is time really the problem? Or are you just being lazy?

Come on. Tell the truth. Are you trying to say that out of 168 hours in a week you can't find four hours to exercise? Who are you kidding? Don't be lazy and don't make excuses. That's against the rules. Exercise. Make the time. No, just do it! You'll feel better. No, really you will. Just do it!

Find Affordable Ways
to Exercise

Your next excuse is bound to be that you can't afford a membership to a gym, what with all the other expenses of being a law student. The rule? You can afford anything you really want. It's called mind over money. But if you're truly strapped for cash, don't despair. Here are alternatives to joining a gym.

Chances are you already have privileges at your school's gym so it won't even cost you any money to work out or swim. If swimming or pumping iron isn't your speed, join a sport team at your school. There's bound to be some kind of team, whether it be softball, basketball, hockey, or skiing. If your school doesn't have any teams, start one. Just get a few people together and work up a sweat a few times per week. It's free. It's a great way to get to know people better. And it's good for your buns.

You hate to sweat? Then get very light ankle weights at a sporting goods store (one-pound weights are ideal for beginners). Strap them onto your ankles and wear them in the house as you go about your chores or during your low-impact aerobic (no-sweat) workout. You can even wear them to class under your jeans in the colder months; or when you're walking to and from the subway, bus, grocery store, or what-have-you. In about a month of constant use, you'll get a nice definition to your thighs and a subtle toning of your buns—all without a single drop of sweat!

If you prefer to sweat, you could invest in a stationary bike, a pair of rollerblades, a good pair of running shoes, or a treadmill. You could buy an exercise tape or video and work up a sweat with Richard Simmons or Gilad—take your pick. You can put one of the Jacksons—Janet or Michael—on the tape deck and dance around your apartment for a half hour three times per week, buck naked. Who would ever guess that you, Mr. or Ms. Dignified-sitting-in-the-third-row-of-the-middle-aisle would ever do a thing like that?

You could go running in the park. Of course, take necessary precautions. A midnight run around New York's Central Park (or whatever park is near you) or some other secluded place might not be a brilliant move, particularly if you're of the female persuasion and you can't kickbox. Speaking of kick-boxing, you could get into the whole Tae Bo craze. That's said to be the hottest exercise for the new millennium.

Another alternative to the gym is going for daily walks on a promenade, or beach, depending on where you live. You can even wake up a little earlier and take the long scenic route to a subway, bus, or railroad, or get off at an earlier stop and walk the rest of the way. Or maybe take up yoga.

None of this grabs you? Then get a tennis partner. Or a squash partner. Play golf. Play badminton. Enroll in ballet class. Enroll in any physical activity class. Enroll in an African-dance class. Do gymnastics. Bellydance. Do calisthenics. Learn to swim. Learn to ice skate. Stretch for fifteen minutes every day. Do one hundred sit-ups every morning before rolling out of bed. Are you getting the idea? Yes? No?! Take up Karate, weight lifting, jogging, walking, running, something! Anything! Hike, bike, blade, sail, box, jump, stomp, romp, stretch, skate, pull, push, crunch, punch your way to a healthy body!

A good workout is empowering. You'll feel like shouting, "I am man/woman, hear me roar!" At the very least, you'll walk with more confidence—and confidence breeds success. And success is sexy.

KNOW YOUR STRESS ZENITH

Depending on your stress zenith—the point at which you're stressed to the max, when you've pretty much become undone, and your face has broken out with a zillion zits (some tea tree oil will zap those hideous monsters to oblivion in no time!)—you're bound to turn into either a skeleton or a blimp. It is very important to keep yourself from reaching this point.

Many law students fall victim to their stress zeniths and begin a downward spiral. It works like this: In addition to being nervous, churning wrecks all the time—to the point that they can't even drink water, or they're eating like King Kong—they unwisely cancel their gym membership because the whole "law school thing" has become undo-able, they're gaining or losing weight (depending on their zenith), and they've even convinced themselves they have no time for anything at all, least of all taking care of themselves!

Don't become a zenith victim. Because you'll burn out by the middle of the semester and become overwhelmed and start talking about how much you hate law school. When you stay clear of your zenith there "ain't no mountain high enough" (least of all Kilimanjaro!) for you to climb because you're strong, you're resilient, your mind is clear, and your buns are tight.

DON'T USE CAFFEINE
OR OTHER DRUGS

"What about caffeine, cigarettes, and an occasional beer?" you ask. Well, let's keep it real. You're an adult. A cup of coffee or a can of beer (assuming you don't drive drunk) probably won't kill you. But it's probably not good for you, either. And smoking, well, that's just bad news. You'll have to decide what's best for you. Just remember that you don't need any of this stuff. You can cope without all of it. In fact, you can cope better without it.

Sleep a Lot

Sleeping is the best way to rejuvenate yourself. Getting enough sleep may not be easy in law school, but try to get as much as you can—especially on weekends.

Getting lots of sleep will help you to cope. So as a rule of thumb, when you're tired, try to call it a night. Then wake up early the next morning and start afresh. Forcing yourself to stay up beyond a certain point is usually counterproductive because your brain shuts off. See, the brain, along with the spinal cord, is our body's center—literally our central nervous system.

When you're tired, it's your brain that's shutting down for the day; it is its way of saying "I'm tired. Let me rest." So, though forcing yourself may work for a few more minutes of semi-productivity, after some time you're better off going to bed. Sometimes being smart means listening to your body and knowing when to say "when."

When you don't know when to say "when," you're simply cutting into time that should have been spent replenishing yourself by sleeping. What ends up happening is that you'll probably oversleep the next morning and end up dragging yourself groggily out of bed. Then you'll inevitably have huge, unsightly bags under your eyes and look like an 85-year-old troll! Then you'll have to have fifteen cups of coffee to function, but you won't be able to function because you'll be totally wired, and your hands will be so shaky you won't be able to hold your pen, and you'll feel absolutely wretched . . . And, good lord, why do that to yourself? Just get enough sleep! (And invest in a soft, feathery pillow.)

LAUGH PLENTY

Laugh, laugh, laugh. Never underestimate the potency of a really good gut laugh. Keeping your sense of humor in law school is crucial. If you don't already have a sense of humor, develop one. But even with the best sense of humor there will be days when you'll want to scream at the world. (Law school can do that to the best of us.)

You literally have to teach yourself to laugh at things. Sometimes, too, you've got to laugh at yourself. Can't laugh? Tickle yourself. Go see a funny movie. Hang out with people who make you feel good and lighthearted. Don't take life or yourself so seriously.

Laughter is a great, safe, enjoyable coping device. It is wonderfully contagious. It is truly one of the best "law school therapies." It sets most people at ease and is one of the easiest nonmedicinal fixes for the frustrations of law school. You're going to get through law school come hell or high water, right? Well, laughter will help you do it. So laugh plenty.

CRY A LITTLE

Crying—like laughing and talking about your problems—is a way to release negative energy. More than likely, you'll cry at least once during law school. Why? Who knows? It's just an emotionally wrenching experience and if you're not too macho, you'll cry. Nothing beats a good cry. Sometimes, it's the only thing that will work. Succumb. Give in with all of your heart. What a stress reliever!

While you should laugh and talk with others, cry in private. Not everyone has to see exactly how overwhelmed you are. The fact is, all law students (especially those in 1L) are just as overwhelmed as you. They may just be better at faking confidence.

Avoid Noisy Roommates

Living comfortably and minimizing the hell of law school means securing a livable environment for yourself. Next to being organized, this is probably the single most important thing you can do as you embark on your law school journey. A comfortable, livable environment means peace of mind. Peace of mind means effective studying, less stress, and more enjoyment of the law school experience.

So forget about living with noisy roommates who drive you nuts with parties till 3:00 in the morning every weekend. Most weekends you'll need to catch up on reading for class, doing your writing or research homework, or simply vegging out. Not that you'll never go to another party again. On the contrary, you might even want to throw one of your own. But you won't have time for parties every single weekend. So don't live with roommates who distract you from your goals.

"Like" Your Mate

Have you ever loved someone but disliked them at the same time? If you're married or living with someone, cohabitating comfortably and minimizing the hell of law school means being with and staying with someone whom you not only love, but also like. And they must like you back, for your sanity's sake.

Also, make sure you and your mate are good "roommates." You need a partner who will pitch in and help out to relieve the stress you're under even if it means doing something simple like fixing themselves a quick meal.

Oh, and you'll have to schedule *everything*, not just when papers are due, but everything, including when you make whoopie. If this sounds cold and calculating, it shouldn't, because it might be the only way to balance all of your competing interests. Otherwise, feelings will get hurt, people will feel neglected, and the frustration levels will mount on both sides. Before you know it, your relationship could be in trouble and, as a result, so will your grades.

CHOOSE NOT TO TANGO

In order for you to cope, you'll need support, understanding, and love. Keep fights with loved ones to a minimum. Be the "bigger" person in your relationships and walk away from minor disputes.

Most fights can be avoided if you let things be. It's hard to fight with someone who won't fight back! Instead of matching a shouting loved one with shouts of your own, speak in a soft, calm voice. It might shame the other person into being more reasonable. Of course, some people just want to fight, no matter how you try to avoid confrontations. You don't need this. You need supportive people around you, not adversaries. Better yet, you need people who understand that a soothing neck massage is what you need after pouring over your books for six and a half hours straight—not a fight over who left the toilet seat up.

The rule is to eliminate distracting, energy-sapping relationships because they are nothing short of academic suicide in law school. Choose not to tango. Build better communication skills with your loved ones. You both will benefit.

FORGET A "PROBLEM SWEETHEART"

Living comfortably and minimizing the hell of law school means having a love interest who understands that you're not always going to have the time to be there for them or to hang out. You can't go to a bar every night like you used to do in college. You're just not going to have the time. You need someone who understands this. Law school is a time-consuming process that takes commitment, focus, drive, and a lot of your free time. Forget about anybody who can't understand this.

Your boyfriend/girlfriend will have to accept that you have to study. If this isn't possible, then you should reevaluate your relationship. What are your needs? What are your partner's needs? Where do you see this relationship going? Is this person helping you or hindering you? Do you really want to be a lawyer? These are some of the questions you must ask yourself. Depending on your answers, you'll know what to do about this "entanglement."

LEAVE HOME

Living comfortably and minimizing the hell of law school means not living with parents and siblings who make you batty, even though you love them and they love you. You can love everybody from afar for three years, can't you? Everybody will survive. But more than that, you'll have some semblance of your sanity left when it's all over. For those of you who are not able to leave the nest, set and stick to some ground rules for your parents and siblings to follow, so that you can maintain a lifestyle that allows you to create the environment you need to succeed in law school.

Although, if you have a perfectly fine relationship with your parents and siblings, and you have total privacy at home, complete with your own wing of the estate, and your siblings are off to Bora Bora to do a three-year thesis on exotic fish, then by all means stay home and save money. Otherwise, consider getting a place of your own.

Keep Good Friends

It helps to have good friends. Make new friends whenever you can; but keep the ones that you've got. Friends help you cope. They help by listening to you, empathizing with you, saying the right things, and just being there. They understand your pain. Sometimes, a friend is easier to talk to than a family member or significant other. So, even though you'll have less time to spend with your friends while you're a law student, don't give them up completely.

Some people, however, sometimes do more harm than good to your psyche—all in the name of friendship. You can't afford this while in law school. Weed out these types of friends. Avoid anyone who is a vexation to your spirit. This is the rule: Only hang around friends who make you feel good about yourself! Reciprocate. This is worth repeating. Only hang around friends who make you feel good about yourself. Reciprocate. And, again, avoid anyone who is a vexation to your spirit.

7

MONEY TIPS

BUDGET WELL

Not only will you have to budget your time, you'll have to budget your money too. Budgeting your money will help you live comfortably without having to worry about too many issues. If you budget well, law school will be more enjoyable.

Budgeting is an easy concept to understand: You have X amount of money that has to be divided into many parts to meet your needs. The more money you have, the more comfortably you can live. You probably won't have a surplus of money when you're a law student, but if you budget well you can do okay. Balance your checkbook. Create a financial plan and stick to it as closely as you can. It will only make your life easier.

TAKE OUT LOANS

If you're in the majority, you'll be financing law school with loans. You're better off not thinking too much about this. Just take out loans for what you need. Tomorrow is another day. When tomorrow comes, you'll pay it all back.

While you should bite the bullet and take out a loan if you need it, you should only borrow as much as you absolutely need. Don't get carried away. Don't take out enough to spend on luxury Carnival Cruises and buy your mother a car or mink. This money isn't free. It's not easy street (even though it may feel like it). You have to pay it all back! And splurging now will simply mean a near-cardiac-arrest-experience when you have your exit loan interview a couple of months before graduation because you will receive your first statement of not only the lump sum you owe, but the monthly payments your lender is expecting—and these payments are going to be big ones, for many, many years! So decide what you can live without. And live without it. That's the crux of budgeting well. (Review Rule 95.)

Maintain Good Credit

One important aspect of budgeting is maintaining a good credit record. The idea is, you can't budget if you've got no money, right? And with bad credit, you won't have money to budget because nobody will be lending you any! So pay your bills on time and keep your charging sprees to a minimum. If you don't, you'll be unable to take out personal loans in the future (law school is three years!).

And if you think that's bad, imagine not being able to get a job or buy a car after you graduate because you have bad credit. You can't even file bankruptcy because student loans have to be paid back. So this is the rule: Safeguard your credit rating at all costs! No lender wants to deal with a "bad credit risk."

APPLY FOR SCHOLARSHIPS

One way to generate extra money (so you can budget well) is to apply for scholarships. Many law students think they don't qualify because of less than stellar grades or LSAT scores. Not necessarily. There are all kinds of scholarships out there. Not all are based on "numerics."

Some scholarships require nothing more than a certain nationality or ethnicity—for example, Italian-Americans who show financial need—or a certain income level, or a certain eye color. Who knows? Go to the Office of Financial Aid. Inquire about what scholarships are offered. Oh, and look at Federal Work-Study and other grants too! There are many of these for which you may qualify and not know. (See the General References appendix for further information.)

SAVE FOR A RAINY DAY

Budgeting well also means saving as much money as you can. There are many ways you can do this even if you don't have a lot to begin with. The following suggestions are hardly exhaustive.

Use coupons when you shop for groceries, make up a grocery list, and shop on weekends. The prices are better so you'll spend less. (Oh, and shop around your neighborhood for the supermarket with the best prices, and always shop there to save money!)

Bag your lunch. Make sandwiches at home instead of buying overpriced, fattening ones at the deli near your school. "I've got no time to make sandwiches in the mornings!" you exclaim. Well, how about making them the night before?

Buy secondhand textbooks instead of new ones. (Much cheaper, sometimes as much as 50%.) And sell yours once you're done with them. Definitely sell all those study guides you bought once you get to 2L, and then to 3L. You'll generate a lot of cash this way.

Shop at thrift shops or designer outlets where you can buy designer clothes, including interview suits, for sometimes up to 70% off department store prices. And, hey, the Salvation

Army sometimes has the most amazing bargains! No one will know where you got your stuff if you don't tell.

Invest in a good, strong, leather book bag that can double as a briefcase, or at the very least, last till the end of your law school career.

Try to save money on leisure activities? For example, if you want to go to the theater as a way of taking a time out, but you can't afford the exorbitant tickets, there's something called the School Theater Ticket Program (they usually have tons of tickets, posters, and programs displayed in the student lounges, or Offices for Students Affairs), where you can get discount tickets by using exchange coupons. In some instances, you can save as much as half the price of the ticket. Why pay full price when you don't have to?

Need more ideas? Buy furniture and other stuff for your apartment at tag sales and garage sales. You can get some great deals this way.

What else? Instead of going to the hairdresser's for a trim every month, have you ever thought of trimming your own hair or getting a friend to trim it for you? If you're a woman of color and you wear braids, learn to braid your locks yourself. This can save you hundreds of dollars every year. Another money-saving tip for women is learning to do your own nails, or go natural—it's healthier anyway because you can pick up a lot of bacteria and infection at these nail salons. Oh, and do you wear glasses or contacts? Most eye-wear stores offer coupons from time to time. Take advantage of these offers. You can get two for the price of one sometimes.

If you can get a nice apartment a half hour from your school at a mere fraction of the price of one that's across the street from your school, take the one a half hour away. Consider the prudence of waking up a measly half hour earlier, especially if you can save an extra $300 per month.

Finally, take public transportation. The money you save on gas, tolls, and parking could be enough to take you to Cancun or Daytona Beach for Spring Break. Wouldn't that be awesome? Or you can use the money to buy yourself a nice stereo or something else for your apartment. You might even use the excess dollars for a year's membership at a gym. Better yet, you can save the excess cash for a rainy day.

8

NETWORKING, SUITS, AND JOBS

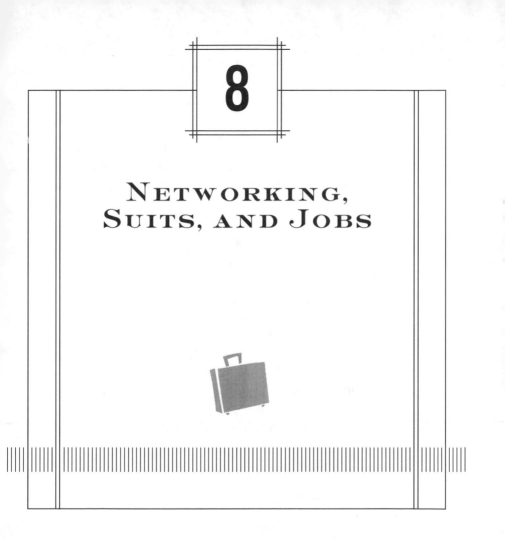

Network

Getting a job is usually the top concern for law students. We all start worrying as early as the summer of the first year of law school. (And believe me, that's not too soon if you don't want to end up temping for a twenty-year-old paralegal who gets a kick out of supervising you as you assemble boxes—for up to two years after you graduate!)

In order to find a job, you may have to call everybody you know. Frequenting your school's career services department may not be enough. You need contacts in this business. So you have to help yourself by doing your own networking. Don't just rely only on "big shot" friends to help you get a job, though. Sometimes the people you think are more likely to help are the least helpful—and vice versa. Treat every occasion and individual as an opportunity to network. Become a social caterpillar. Smile, charm, and smooze. Flatter, beguile, and captivate. And carry business cards and tic tacs . . . Just in case. You never know who can help you.

GET TO KNOW YOUR NEIGHBORS

The people in your community are worth getting to know. They may be important connections for your future job searches. The man who owns the neighborhood deli might have an attorney who needs an intern for the summer and a full-time associate in the fall after graduation. You never know. So always be friendly and approachable to people in your neighborhood. Treat your neighbors with respect. The idea here is not to be a fraud but to simply embrace the idea of community. Don't alienate all your neighbors by holding wild parties every weekend (as if you have time!). Don't scream nasty expletives at the neighborhood butcher just because he "cut your beef diagonally instead of in squares like you told him to five times!" Don't drive like a maniac through the neighborhood streets. Act like an intelligent, well-mannered adult.

And while you're getting to know people, don't rule out occasions such as weddings and any and all social functions. Oh, and the judge who sits in the back pew of your church every Sunday could very well be an important contact (he could write a recommendation for you) when you begin your job search. So be respectful. People notice when you're not.

Invest in a Dark Suit

A dark suit is an absolute must. You'll be interviewing as early as January of the spring semester of 1L for summer internships with judges or law firms. So you'll have to have a dark suit as early as then. Why a dark suit as opposed to a light one? Because dark suits look more commanding than light-colored ones. And most lawyers wear dark-colored suits. Navy ones in particular. So buy yourself a navy, gray, or black suit. Make sure it fits well. Women, watch your skirt lengths. Your skirt should hover around your knees. Men, make sure your shirts are nicely pressed. And everybody should go light on the fragrances, okay?!

DON'T WORK

It's absolutely recommended that you *not* work in the first year of law school if you can avoid it. Work during your summer vacation of the first year.

After the first year you'll have a bit more flexibility. You'll feel more in control and know what to expect. You can get a part-time job then. But only a part-time job. For those of you who must work full time, let me be the first to congratulate you on your superior strength, brains, and moxie. You'll usually take only one less class than full-time students. Plus you'll be holding down a full-time job. This will be a great challenge. However, others have done it, so it *is* do-able. But it will be tough. Good luck to you. You'll need it.

BECOME YOUR PROFESSOR'S RESEARCH ASSISTANT

One of the high points of any student's law school career is being asked by their favorite professor to be their research assistant. Imagine your surprise when you check your mail-folder or your voice mail and discover a message from the professor you've been in awe of, asking you to be their assistant! There is no greater honor. You're bound to be unable to contain yourself and will be bursting with joy for a good three weeks at least.

The rule is: You're allowed to grin from ear to ear if that's how you feel. This is one of the few times when you're allowed to gush when dealing with your professor. Go ahead and lavishly compliment your professor on how phenomenal you think she or he is. Then take a couple of days more to float on your cloud. Then break a leg!

Consider a Judicial Internship

If you're willing to forego a salary, volunteer with a judge for the summer. Next to studying abroad, or being your favorite professor's research assistant, a judicial internship is probably the best law school summer experience. The knowledge you'll acquire by interning far makes up for the lack of compensation.

Always look and act like a lawyer. That means wear a navy suit and pretend you're it. Don't blow your credibility by showing up to the court dressed like you're heading to the beach.

As you would for any other job interview, give a firm handshake, make eye contact, and thank the judge profusely for meeting with you. The handshake doesn't have to be so firm that it rattles the judge's cheeks, but it shouldn't be wimpy either. And you don't have to gush when you thank the judge for meeting with you, but show your appreciation for their time. Always maintain a level of professionalism.

One major perk that might make up for the loss of a salary is that you get to meet a lot of attorneys while interning for a judge. These might be excellent future contacts. Thus, don't underestimate the importance of stepping up to and dressing for the occasion. Nothing will feel nicer than when another judge or attorney mistakes *you* for an attorney!

VOLUNTEER WITH A
SMALL LAW FIRM

If all else fails and you didn't find a summer job in the time you allotted yourself, check out your school's career services department. Law firms are always looking for students who want to volunteer their time. The first place they start looking is the career services center of a law school.

Also, agencies that specialize in civil-rights cases and other pro bono work—such as legal aid societies—always need student volunteers. Other public-interest groups like the Civil Liberties Union often need student volunteers too. You might want to consider these volunteer possibilities as ways to meet attorneys and build your resume.

9

Simple
Pleasures

RENT YOUR OWN
SHANGRI-LA!

Renting your own place now might be just what the doctor ordered. If you don't have substantial savings in the bank, didn't get a full scholarship, and you're not the sole heir of a rich uncle in Tennessee who will croak on cue, take out enough loans to cover living expenses and rent an apartment or room of your own.

Yes, you'll probably be $100,000 in the hole when you're through with law school, but the peace of mind is worth every penny. Hey, live in the moment! Be prudent, of course (see Rule 95: Budget Well), but let three years from now take care of itself—in terms of paying it all back, that is.

Just think. For three short years you can have your own Utopia—flat, studio, or chalet—where you can create the living environment you've always wanted. Your very own Shangri-La!

RULE 108

USE AROMATHERAPY TO
IMPROVE YOUR MEMORY

Creating a pleasant aroma in your surroundings can help you handle the stresses of law school better. No, really! Pleasing aromas have been proven to make people feel better about their lives in general. In fact, experts say that aromatherapy is good for the soul because it promotes a sense of well-being, reduces stress, and improves memory. What could be better for a law student? Surely being immersed in a pleasant-smelling Shangri-La (versus, say, being immersed in the odor of smelly sneakers) can't hurt, right?

Oh, but of course you don't have time to go to exotic aroma shops searching for scented oils, candles, lotions, potions, and potpourri. This is the rule: Buy air fresheners (the ones you stick up) at the supermarket every few weeks and place them all over your apartment. Make sure you put one over your bed where it's the last thing you smell at night and the first thing you wake up to in the morning. When the scent starts to wane, get fresh ones. It's that simple.

MAKE LOTS OF WHOOPIE!

Why not indulge in some safe, sweet, utterly climactic "you-know-what" at least once per week? (And even if you don't have a partner to indulge in this you-know-what, there are many ways to skin a cat!) Need incentives to indulge in this, quote-end-quote, you-know-what? It's a great stress reliever. It's good for your complexion. It's good for your psyche. You need it. You deserve it—at least once in a while! So do it! Make time. Pencil in sessions on your organization calendar. Yes, he or she may not like being penciled in, but what's the alternative? Becoming completely unraveled by all these competing interests? Losing your sanity?

But if you are going to pleasure yourself by "making whoopie!" there are two rules: First, make it safe by using all necessary precautions. (For some crazy reason, the word *monogamy* comes to mind.) And second, it must be *climactic*.

TAKE SOOTHING BATHS

Law school life should be full of simple, mindless, little pleasures. One such pleasure is taking soothing bubble baths. What decadence, you say! But you're worth it. And you deserve it. You can allow yourself this little treat once per week. (Perhaps after making whoopie!)

If you look at it as a reward, spending a half hour immersed in fluffy suds won't seem so extravagant at all. It'll just seem natural, like the least you can do for yourself after accomplishing all your goals the previous week. What might be a tad extravagant is pouring a gallon of milk and a few petals from a rose in the water—in addition to all the other bubbly bath products that you're bound to use to pamper yourself. But why not? Life is short. Oh, and don't forget to jot these "bath" sessions down on your academic calendar. You don't want to throw your organization chart askew just to frolic in soap bubbles.

KEEP A LAW SCHOOL JOURNAL

Why not keep a journal so that you can capture, forever, this unforgettable experience? Imagine the value to posterity? It would be great, wouldn't it, to be able to pick up your journal three years from now and laugh at your insecurities, or smile at your courage while you were plodding along through the law school maze? You probably won't believe how much you've changed. But a more immediate perk is, keeping a journal will help you keep things in perspective, thus your life will be easier.

Journaling doesn't have to be a big production. All you have to do is quickly jot down the day's events on a single page, or a fraction of a page, when time permits.

Adopt a Pet

A pet might be just what you need. Tell the truth: Haven't you always wanted a parrot so you could teach it shocking expletives? (Shame on you!) Well now's the time to get your parrot because, in law school, you'll be using the most shocking expletives you've ever used in your life!

"I don't like parrots!" you yell hotly. Well, there are so many other pets to choose from, my dear. There is the proverbial pig named "Babe." Or you could get a hamster, gerbil, boa constrictor, turtledove, bird, lizard, or frog. You might even get a rabbit or a peacock. How about an ant colony to indulge the scientist in you? How about a chimp? No? Okay, a dog? Maybe a cat? No?! What about a plant? Hey, plants can be pets too!

Whatever you do, remember that you're known by the pets you keep. So this is the rule: Make sure it's legal to own this animal as a pet before you get it. You'll want to be a member of your state bar, not have a gavel come down on you for having broken the law. And most importantly, you'll have to devote time and care to your pet, especially if you've adopted a cat or dog. And remember that a pet is a family member and can be your best friend and companion when times get rough. Ask any pet owner.

CULTIVATE A HOBBY

Hobbies are relaxing and you need all the relaxation you can get while in law school. Hobbies should never feel like work. In fact, if your hobby feels like work to you, don't do it. It's probably not your forte. The rule is to do something for your own relaxation, something mindless that you enjoy doing just for the fun of it. The fun is in the trying, and this activity will free your mind from everyday thoughts and troubles.

What can you do? Perhaps you could take up gardening. Become a full-fledged gardener. Even if you can't have an outdoor garden, create one in the corner of your living room. Get a collection of plants to nurture and put them on your windowsills. Talk to your plants and flowers every day so that they will feel loved and grow. When the pressures of law school get to you, take time out and look at your garden, while breathing in and out deeply (perhaps this is a good time to do your visualization exercises—see Rules 12 and 13).

Or, perhaps you could devote a couple of hours per week to writing a novel or something wild like that. This might sound like a lot of work, but it can be accomplished at your very own leisure, thank-you-very-much. Don't give yourself deadlines. Just write when the mood strikes and when time permits.

If writing doesn't do it for you, people watching, for example, is the cheapest hobby ever. In fact, it's the best. It costs nothing at all! All it requires is some time and a public place.

What else? You could try your hand at sculpting, learning a foreign language, or playing the guitar. Okay, so your guitar will end up collecting dust in a corner of your bedroom in no time. And you just don't have a knack for foreign languages and will never be fluent in anything but your native tongue. And the only thing you'll ever successfully sculpt is a few balls of clay.

So what? Why not make a hobby out of trying new things? You can take all these classes through continuing education programs, available at any local high school, college, or YMCA. Usually $50.00 pays for a three-month course. And as an added bonus, you get to meet a lot of different people, most of whom are professionals like yourself looking for a breather and/or romantic interest.

Add Hobbies to Your Resume

The wonderful thing about hobbies is that they're fun. You need that in law school. But did you know that a hobby is something you can also add to your resume when you start looking for a job? Having a hobby says a lot about you. It makes you appear as a well-rounded, interesting person and not just a walking legal reporter. So show prospective employers that you have a pulse and that it throbs. Get a hobby!

Rule of thumb: Don't put a hobby on your resume if you don't know enough about it to carry on a conversation. Remember that whatever you put on your resume is fair game for questioning on an interview. Don't say you're an avid stamp collector if you don't collect stamps. The person interviewing you might have "written the book" on stamp collecting or may be a collector. They might even have given you the interview based on this seemingly trivial bit of information you included on your resume. Be careful.

Throw a Party

A party is a great way to get to know your new classmates and release law school stress. Why not throw one? You don't have to have a grand excuse. Have one just *because!* If for no other reason, throw a party to prevent the law school blahs from driving you out of your cotton-picking mind. Break up the monotony of casebooks and tyrant professors. Do it!

Oh, and you don't have to have a big bash with tons of people. If you only have a tiny studio apartment, for instance, you can invite six people over for crackers, Brie, and really cheap wine. Most people will offer to bring something so spending hundreds of dollars is unnecessary. There are no rules except you can't talk about law school.

If, however, you feel throwing a party during the semester is too frivolous an undertaking for a serious law student like yourself, you can throw one during winter or summer recess. Better yet, leave law school with a bang! Throw your party in the last semester of your third year. That's probably the best time because you'll know who your law school friends really are by then. They will be the ones who stuck with you through thick and thin. What better way to say good-bye and good luck to your true friends?

EPILOGUE

I've tried to share everything I think might help you deal with the "small stuff" of law school, to keep it from mushrooming into "big stuff" and ruining what can be a rich, rewarding experience. Please keep in mind that you should premise everything I've said with the phrase, "I must always do what's best for me!" Remember also to always strive for balance, and to believe in yourself no matter what—because you can do it!

Three years from your first day of classes, you'll be standing—victorious—on the top of "Kilimanjaro." No one can accuse you then of being anything less than a champion. As Theodore Roosevelt said, you're no "poor spirit who neither enjoys much nor suffers much." Neither can anyone accuse you of "living in the gray twilight that knows not victory nor defeat." But, boy, will you ever relish the taste of victory standing proud as you will on graduation day at the top of Kilimanjaro. (See Rule 1.) Looking down from your lofty height, you'll say: "Hey, mountain (you son-of-a-gun!), I think I've just reached the top." And Kilimanjaro will respond somewhat grudgingly, of course (after all, didn't she taunt you every step of the way?), "Hey, you! Congratulations on a job well done!"

Good luck!

SUGGESTED READING LIST

The following is a list of books that will be helpful. You probably won't have time to read them all, but try to read as many of them as you can. They cover tips on surviving law school; improving your legal writing and research—crucial undertakings for every law student; a couple of major law suits (as in *A Civil Action* and *The Buffalo Creek Disaster*) that you might find interesting; and other pertinent topics.

Barbri First Year Survival Manual, Richard J. Conviser. The Barbri Group, 1997, 1st edition.

Blacks Law Dictionary, Henry Campbell Black. West Publishing Company, 1990, 6th edition.

The Buffalo Creek Disaster, Gerald M. Stern. Vintage Books, 1977, 1st edition.

A Civil Action, Jonathan Harr. Vintage, 1997, 1st edition.

The Complete Law School Companion, Jeff Deaver. John Wiley & Sons, Inc., 1992, 2nd edition.

Drafting Legal Documents, Barbara Child. West Publishing Co., 1992, 2nd edition.

Guide to Law Schools, Introduction by Professor Gary A. Munneke (Pace University School of Law School). Barron's Educational Series, Inc., 1998, 13th edition.

How to Succeed in Law School, Professor Gary A. Munneke. Barron's Educational Series, Inc. 1994, 1st Edition.

Inside the Law Schools: A Guide by Students for Students, Sally Goldfarb. E.P. Dutton, 1986, 4th edition.

Introduction to Study and Practice of Law, Kenney Hegland. West Publishing Co., 1995, 2nd edition.

Law School Companion, Paul M. Lisner, Steven Friedland, and Chris Salamone. Random House, The Princeton Review, 1995, 1st edition.

Lexis-Nexis for Law Students, Stephen L. Emanuel. Imanuel Law Outlines, Inc., 1995, 2nd edition.

Looking at Law School, Stephen Gillers. A Meridian Book, 1997, 4th edition.

One L, Scott Turow. Warner Books, 1988, 1st edition.

Strategies & Tactics for First Year Law, Kimm Alayne Walton. Emanuel Law Outlines, Inc., 1995, 1st edition.

29 Reasons Not to Go to Law School, Ralph Warner, Toni Ihara, and Barbara Kate Repa. Nolo Press, 1996, 4th edition.

Women in Legal Education: A Comparison of the Law School Performance and Law School Experiences of Women and Men, Linda F. Wightman. From the Law School Admission Council Research Report Series, 1996.

Writing and Analysis in the Law, Helene S. Shapo, Marilyn R. Walter, and Elizabeth Fajans. Foundation Press, 1995, 3rd edition.

GENERAL REFERENCES

The Sentry Student Security Plan is a college health insurance program for all students, their dependents, and spouses. It is administered nationally by E.J. Smith & Associates, Inc., E.J. Smith Insurance Agency 899 Skokie Boulevard, Northbrook, IL 60062-4024 (847/564-3660).

The Student is a dental insurance plan administered by New York University College of Dentistry, 345 East 24th Street, Room 191W, New York, NY 10160-0331 (212/998-9912).

The American Bar Association Student Insurance is a medical insurance plan. You may write or call them at P.O. Box 809025, Dallas, TX 75380-9025 (800/505-5450; 972/233-8200 or e-mail: INFO@SID.COM).

The National Student Services, Inc. may be reached at P.O. Box 2137, Stillwater, OK 74076 (800/256-6774; 800/677-0215). This is a property insurance plan designed to protect the personal property of students (such as laptops, clothing, books) from all sorts of casualties like fire or theft.

Ask for the **Grants Register** at your financial aid office. It's a complete guide to post-graduate funding—an alphabetical listing of over 2,600 awards for which you might be eligible—that could help you reduce your astronomical tuition bills.

The Nestle U.S.A. Minority Scholarships. If you're female or minority, find out about these scholarships. You may qualify for one of them. Write to Nestle U.S.A. Community Affairs Dept., 800 North Brand Blvd., Glendale, CA 91203.

Contact **PMBR** when you begin preparing for the bar (800/523-0777). It's a supplemental program to the other bar review courses. PMBR specializes in preparing students for the MBE (the uniform, national 200-question multiple-choice exam). Most students who take it swear that it's worth the investment.

If you would like to tell me how you feel about my book,
or would like to suggest even more rules to help law students,
please write to me in care of my publisher:

HARMONY BOOKS
201 East 50th Street
New York, New York 10022

THE PRINCETON REVIEW

GET INTO THE LAW SCHOOL
OF YOUR CHOICE

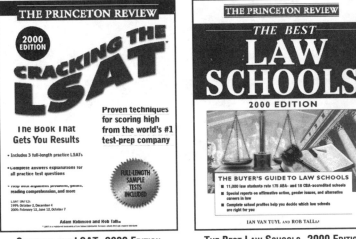

CRACKING THE LSAT, 2000 EDITION
0-375-75409-1 • $20.00

THE BEST LAW SCHOOLS, 2000 EDITION
0-375-75464-4 • $20.00